Surge: Draf[

RACHEL BLAU DUPLESSIS is a U.S. po[___ ___ ___ ___y
is the subject of an on-line colloquium and set of essays published in
Jacket2 in December 2011 jacket2.org/feature/drafting-beyond-ending

Her recent critical work *Purple Passages: Pound, Eliot, Zukofsky, Olson, Creeley and the Ends of Patriarchal Poetry* (University of Iowa Press, 2012) is part of a feminist trilogy of works about gender and poetics that includes *The Pink Guitar: Writing as Feminist Practice* and *Blue Studios: Poetry and its Cultural Work*, both from University of Alabama Press. DuPlessis is also the author of *Genders, Races, and Religious Cultures in Modern American Poetry, 1908–1934* (Cambridge University Press, 2001).

In 2013 *Brouillons* (comprising twenty drafts) translated by Auxeméry will appear from José Corti (Paris). Also in 2013, a translation of *Dieci Bozze* translated into Italian by Renata Morresi has been published by Vydia Editions. An Italian chapbook of Draft 111 has been issued by La Camera Verde.

In early 2012, DuPlessis was a Distinguished Visitor in the English Department at the University of Auckland. DuPlessis has held an appointment to the National Humanities Center in North Carolina in 2008–09. In 2007, she was awarded a residency for poetry at Bellagio, sponsored by the Rockefeller Foundation. In 2002, she received a Pew Fellowship in the Arts; also in 2002, she was awarded the third Roy Harvey Pearce / Archive for New Poetry Prize.

Also by Rachel Blau DuPlessis from Salt

Drafts: Drafts 39–57, *Pledge, with Draft, unnumbered: Précis* (Salt, 2004)
Torques: Drafts 58–76 (Salt, 2007)
Pitch: Drafts 77–95 (Salt, 2010)
The Collage Poems of Drafts (Salt, 2011)

Surge: Drafts 96–114

by

RACHEL BLAU DUPLESSIS

SALT

CROMER

PUBLISHED BY SALT PUBLISHING

12 Norwich Road, Cromer Norfolk NR27 0AX, United Kingdom

Salt Publishing 2013

Printed and bound in the United States by Lightning Source Inc

Typeset in Swift 9.5 / 13

ISBN 978 1 84471 944 0 paperback

1 3 5 7 9 8 6 4 2

Contents

Acknowledgments

My first and heartfelt acknowledgment is to Chris Hamilton-Emery of Salt Publishing for his commitment to this work as a whole. I am also notably grateful to the editors and others named below for their serious interest in Drafts.

Cover. Collage by RBD. I thought the citation was by John Cage. Apparently not.

Preface.

This text was written in June and early July 2012, with thanks for their very helpful responses to Libbie Rifkin and Patrick Pritchett. The statement cribs a few paragraphs from my work "Reflections of the Long Poem: Autobiography of a Practice," delivered in a variety of venues, from University of Kansas to University of Auckland (as well as Universities of Sydney, Otago, Ryerson, and Guelph). Some remarks on the objectivists come from a conference on New Objectivism, delivered in Rome, May 2012. Some remarks on female authorship also appear in the Bergvall, Browne, Carmody, Place anthology (see Draft 98).

Draft 96: Velocity
All Together Now: A Digital Bridge for Auckland and Sydney, 2010. Pam Brown. Martin Edmond, Brian Flaherty, and Michele Leggott eds.
http://www.nzepc.auckland.ac.nz/features/home&away/duplessis-sydney.asp

This work appears as a chapbook made by Dawn Prendergast, published 2011, from Little Red Leaves.

Draft 97: Rubrics
Blackbox Manifold 3 (Summer 2009), Alex Houen and Adam Piette, eds.. http://www.manifold.group.shef.ac.uk/

Draft 98: Canzone
This poem appeared in *Jacket Magazine* 38 (Fall 2009), John Tranter, ed.

http://jacketmagazine.com/38/duplessis-draft98l.shtml

The poem, with its accompanying comments "Driven To Torque Texts: Appropriation and Dante," appeared in *"I'll Drown My Book": Conceptual Writing by Women*. Caroline Bergvall, Laynie Browne, Teresa Carmody, Vanessa Place, eds. Los Angeles: Les Figues Press, 2012.

This poem will appear in *Brouillons*, trans. Auxeméry from José Corti, 2013.

This poem appears in *Dieci Bozze* from Vydia editions, translated by Renata Morresi.

Draft 99: Intransitive
This poem first appeared in *Jacket Magazine* 38 (Fall 2009). Thanks to John Tranter for generously enduring its complexities of formatting.

http://jacketmagazine.com/38/duplessis-draft99redacted.shtml

This poem will appear in *Brouillons*, trans. Auxeméry from José Corti, 2013.

Draft 100: Gap
Conjunctions (Fall 2009): 331–35. Bradford Morrow, ed.

Draft 101: Puppet Opera
Published in *ESQUE* 1(September 2010), Amy King and Ana Boži evi eds. http://www.wix.com/poetries/esque1#!issue1-ifesto/vstc3=page-5

This work was also performed at the 2011 Poets Theater Festival sponsored by Small Press Traffic.

Draft 102: One-on-One. *Cambridge Literary Review* 4 (2011): 20–25, in a section selected by Emily Critchley.

Draft 103: Punctum. *VLAK* 1. 1 (Sept. 2010): 100–115. Louis Armand, Carol Watts, Eddie Berrigan, eds.

Draft 104: The Book. *Cambridge Literary Review* 4 (2011): 26–29. Also in Critiphoria, March 2010 http://www.critiphoria.org/Issue2/Rachel_Blau_DuPlessis_Issue2.pdf
This poem will appear in *Brouillons*, trans. Auxeméry from Jose Corti, 2013.

Draft 105: Pilgrimage.
Hambone 20 (2012): 63–66. Nathaniel Mackey, ed.

Draft 106: Words. *Aufgabe* #12, forthcoming.

Draft 107: Meant to say.
Slightly revised after first publication. Thanks to Tom Devaney for his reading. *Aufgabe* #10. 2010. E. Tracy Grinnell, ed.

Appearing in both English and Italian in EX.IT, translated by Renata Morresi (2013).

Draft 108: Ballad and Gloss
As a Little Red Leaves Chapbook, published December 2012, with thanks to Dawn Prendergast.

Draft 109: Wall Newspaper.
Thanks to Aldon Nielsen for help with a specific reference and to both Peter and Meredith Quartermain for their responses. This poem appeared in *Jacket2*, in the feature on RBD called Drafting Beyond the Ending, curated by Patrick Pritchett. December 2011.
http://jacket2.org/feature/drafting-beyond-ending

Draft CX: Primer. Only the short preface to Draft CX: Primer is re-published here. Along with Draft 94: Mail Art, the work called Primer appears in full in *The Collage Poems of Drafts*, published by Salt Publishing, 2011. The collage poems F, I, J, K, & Y in *Dear Navigator* Five collage poems http://www.saic.edu/dearnavigator

The collage poems B, Q, T, X, Z in B&W in *VIZ. Inter-Art*. Roxi Powers Hamilton, ed., forthcoming.

Draft 111: Arte Povera
Feminist Studies 38.3 (Fall 2012) in a special grouping of work by former editors and members of the *Feminist Studies* editorial collective in honor of Claire Moses, who was for many years the journal's managing editor. There are some differences in the text of this first publication and the book version.

Also as a chapbook in Italian, La Camera Verde 2013, translated by Renata Morresi.

Draft 112: Verge
Alligatorzine, June 2012. Kurt Devrese, ed. www.alligatorzine.be/pages/101/zine131.html

For the experiences that led to this poem, I am grateful to the hospitality of Evy Varsamopoulou and others.

Draft 113: Index.
Poetry Project Newsletter, October/November 2012, with thanks to Paul Foster Johnson, ed. Backstory: In 2006, Jim Carpenter, applications-development consultant and lecturer in computer programming and systems design at The Wharton School, University of Pennsylvania, constructed a set of word frequency data (with statistical breakouts) on the first 57 Drafts. I thank him for satisfying our mutual curiosity—each for quite different purposes. Some of his findings helped this poem. I am also very grateful to the group of committed writers for the *Jacket2* feature on my work

posted December 14, 2011, who collectively confirmed some of the observations presented here.

Draft 114: Exergue and Volta.
Not previously published.
Warm thanks to Ron Silliman and to Meredith Quartermain for a mid-writing response to this poem. I extend great thanks to Michele Leggott and her request in 2008 that I "fill" a Tapa Notebook, where a few sections were first sketched. This Tapa Notebook is now held in Special Collections, The University of Auckland Library, New Zealand as DuPlessis, *NZ notebook*, 2008. University of Auckland nzepc records. MSS & Archives 2003/4, item 3/13.

Preface to Surge: Drafts 96–114

My poems since 1986 are part of one large work called *Drafts*. In 2012, this work reached the numerical goal that I had established in 1993. This book, *Surge,* contains the "final" poem, "Draft 114: Exergue and Volta," bringing the total number of poems to 114/115 — a double indicator. The numerical ambiguity occurs because of the unnumbered poem placed in the middle of this work, a poem itself comprised of 57 short poems (alluding to sonnets) that "summarize" (with a mis-en-abyme-ish twist) the first fifty-seven poems in the series.

A reader might ask why — with my open-ended ethos, or with my allusive relations to certain long poems themselves in the realm of the unfinished — did I project any terminus to *Drafts*? Isn't this a contravention of the fundamental terms of the poem? Is it not an "endless poem"? Well, yes, it is in my mind, and the poem manifests an endless dialogue between closed and open. But it has been useful to me to have a sense of scale (this terminus at 114) in which folding up *Drafts* into itself and not writing more of this exact work (but of some related, as yet undefined poems) became a plausible outcome of my having written this in the first place. When I began *Drafts*, I wrote the poems by going one to one to one. But soon enough other patterns began loosely to establish themselves. This preface gives an account of some of those patterns — by which I mean some of these choices.

During the poem's long unfolding. I invented a structure for *Drafts* by attending heuristically to the feeling of the parts and to my fascinated consideration of their necessity. *Drafts* does not have an indeterminate structure, but it does do two opposite things at once — "A" and "not-A." I don't mean to evoke Louis Zukofsky's long poem in this phrase (though the allusion is amusing, after all). I mean, my poem is both A and not-A in its mechanisms — a fact said to be technically or philosophically illogical. This in itself is very pleasurable. *Drafts* closes without ending. I mean it — *Drafts* ends, but doesn't end. It is not teleological, but has stopping places. Many. One can begin anywhere and read in any desired direction. It is both a constellation and a set with many series in it.

[1]

Drafts has occupied this double terrain—open and closed, A and not-A—throughout the many years of its construction. That is, it attempts, structurally and in its poetics, to over-pass any number of opposites. This work is conceptual and expressive, odd and even, ending and not ending. The work comprises individual poems to be read separately and poems in a communal setting that, like any grouping, is both integrated and not-integrated, melding and jostling. The poem *Drafts* is expressive (not in an exclusively personal sense) and conceptual; it has collage juxtapositions and syntactic connections. . . . the list could go on. By making *The Collage Poems* (published as a visual book in 2011) I both broke with the solely verbal aspect of this text and ruptured the insistence on 19 poems (or a multiple) per codex, by having two works put together in a separate book that bridged—or leveraged interstitial space between—two groups of drafts. *Drafts* has made a structure where you cannot say which text has priority, that is, which text glosses and which text states, which is the original and which is the elaboration. I wanted the sections to be self-contained, each readable on its own, and readable in any order. I also wanted an un-totalized total number. Is all that self-contradictory? The long poem gets beyond the concept "self-contradictory" (perhaps to achieve the apogee of the poly-contradictory). So it is an anti-totalizing text in a situation with totalizing temptations. An anti-high-modernist text within modernist modernity and its long, lively aftermath. *Drafts* is a work that as a whole ruptures the binaries that might contain it.

Hence *Drafts* offers a third way. A tertium quid. Something un-binarist. It will go on, but in another mode. H.D. said it—but in her more contained context of mythic repetition:

the same—different—the same attributes,
different yet the same as before.
        H.D. *Trilogy* III

The endless poem was a phrase that I found early in my career. As a concept, it offers many possibilities.

∽

In about 2008, a potential (and in fact unused) title for a particular Draft was given to me in a dream in which I was "explaining" all of *Drafts* to someone. Now images are sometimes given to me in a dream, but I have never had one word or even any writing emerge in that zone. For me, dream writing—writing seen or held in a dream— is unreadable or evanescent (as my section in "Draft 23: Findings" stated, while I was trying to parse an imaginary letter I had received from the then dead Leland Hickman). So this event was odd. The title given to me was "obbligato." It is the older or formal Italian word for "thank you." And like the current word in Portuguese—"obrigado"—it really means "obliged to you," or as we used to say in English "much obliged." I took this dream word as expressing my thanks to whatever universe allowed me to do whatever I have done with *Drafts*. But it turns out (cunning dream) that this word is a pun on (and variant spelling of) obligato / obbligato, a musical term that means "not to be left out, indispensable" and is said of an accompaniment that is an integral part of a piece. The etymology of this word goes to the word *ligare*, meaning to bind. I know I am bound to this poem and to the pulse of generativity that it has manifested for 26 years. If more is obbligato—required, I will go forward (with gratitude) into another mysterious terrain, in deference to and in relation to the mystery that has always generated the poem. Perhaps the words for this mystery are IT and IS. These poems have, at any rate, returned to those concepts as an insistent continuo—or obbligato.

∽

The term and concept *Drafts* offered a prompt to writing. The word stated that every individual poem was in some sense provisional. Of course given the title word "drafts," the work was structured to continue for a good long while in order to illustrate and enact the fact that every poem is not quite it. That is, each poem lacks being the definitive poem; it is just a "draft." I can't see that "Draft 114: Exergue and Volta" is any more definitive just because it is the declared stopping place. In many ways, it is doomed to be even less definitive than other ones. Really the metaphoric idea of *Drafts* was to write a poem in which every section was as if an incomplete attempt at the same poem; hence failure is part of the writing system—indeed, central to it. For this magical, imagined fullest poem is nonetheless always impossible, always implausible, and therefore necessarily always deferred. Far from the Mallarmean idea that the whole of the universe would end up in a book, it is exactly and exactly not that Mallarmean idea. I mean that all the poems are self-different although patterned, and so it is an illusion that they are "one" poem; on the other hand, it appears as if I am writing figurations that will never appear but are everywhere sensed in various avatars. The relationship of these prefigurations to an endlessly deferred secular concept of presence suggests itself. "So that the whole, someone might say, is one poem articulated a hundred-odd ways, yet, at the same time, the whole is so many different works that it cannot be unified or accounted for. This could be called a failure. I mean a pleasure. (Precisely to have failure—on that scale and with that level of stubbornness—was one of the few things I foresaw.)" (*Torques*, 135; section 18 of "Draft 76; Work Table with Scale Models")

∿

Typos for the word Draft before being corrected by the author include
    Daft
    Drat
    Raft

[4]

~

As for the long poem and its numerology—long poem writers do count. They count things that other people might not count. They think as they count, and the thinking concerns structural shapes and their possible meanings. They make structures of numbers. This is a charm of control (even a mini-obsession?) in a situation rapidly becoming more and more wayward, vast, extensive, and virtually out of control because of the growing scale of the long poem as sections get added to it. The counting—the commitment to this count, a count I had committed to (this is a tautology)—would have been undermined had I not proposed the "end" of this phase of the project. The quondam shapeliness of the numerical plan plus the "ungainliness" that the epigraph from Zukofsky heralded are, together, part of the practice. The motif "how even is with odd" announced itself early (in "Draft 6: Midrush," *Toll*, 38), and the numerical goal offered a structural version of "how even is with odd." So I said 114 poems, but there will always be one more—the unnumbered draft, driven into the middle of the poem like a marker, and which considers half of the poem (the half that was written, for which there is therefore, a "Précis") while of course unable to do anything at all with the 57 poems that were, at that moment, unwritten. That ungainly shapeliness and unsymmetrical symmetry, the result of a series of on-the-ground construction choices, would have disappeared had I simply written 115, 116, 117 and so on, continuing in a row after 114.

~

It is true that, in this mumbling over numbers that any long poem writer perforce does, if I had seven (rather than six) passes of 19, there would be oddness for sure, but no evenness. Once I had decided this—a mysterious decision—I thought that the 114 / 115 balance (which is an even number and an odd number) around a "Précis" was an interesting idea, almost a duck/rabbit, both/and pattern. Is it

[5]

symmetry or not-symmetry? I created symmetry and the thematic/ structural oddity of summarizing half the poem in the unnumbered poem (summarizing 1–57 in the Précis), and then leaving the other half blank. This half-yes, half-no pattern was enormously satisfying to me, a sense of unaccountable mystery deep within the work as a whole. (The work began, after all, with the letter N, and the first poem ended evoking the letter Y.) This effect would not have been possible had I simply continued.

Also, dear reader, the question of death or inability is not unrealistic when one is lucky enough to have reached a certain age. One cannot dwell on this, but one often tries to "account" for it (there's another count). I wanted to have *my* say on *Drafts*. And so this book ends with "Draft 114: Exergue and Volta." I have spoken about my desire to reach this 114th poem, but I have simultaneously spoken about a desire to "fold up"—not to complete—*Drafts*. So "final poem" is clearly a metaphor for "not final." It is almost unbelievable that the project was so generative, so sustaining, for so many years. My basic emotions when faced with this whole work are passion and gratitude.

~

The work can be read numerically, in the order of writing, or even chronologically in order of writing (these two not always exactly the same). But that order is not emphasized as contributing to structure or findings. The work as a whole is not a sequence but a modular series. It is an anti-patriarchal maze with many threads. One can begin anywhere and read in any desired direction. This like the antic way Dorothy Richardson once described her reading of novels—cutting random pages of random books that were staged all over her house. The poem also exemplifies Gertrude Stein's "beginning again and again," (as well as evoking a version of "using everything") while not necessarily desiring to be Steinian. The reader cannot physically rearrange the numerical order of the poems (as

[6]

might be possible were the poem approached like Robert Grenier's "box"), but her reading is not controlled by it.

~

Between Draft 19 and Draft 20, about seven years into the project, it occurred to me that I did not have to go endlessly one to one to one, like one of those spool-yarn projects that children sometimes take on — leaving them with a long strand of knitted length and the question what to do with it. Instead, I could begin again. Thus I decided to repeat some version of these themes and materials in the same general order every nineteen poems, folding one group over another, making new works but works evoking motifs and themes in the former one — and also, of course, generating new images, materials and themes as I went. The realization that I could make a recurrent but free structure via a fold happened in a sudden flash (like most of my structural insights), and the thought delivered a fantastic if then unsorted set of formal and intellectual implications all at once, like an avalanche of scree rushing down a mountain.

The interplay between sameness and difference constructs a profound structure of feeling about memory and loss, about recurrence and the unique instance, about fresh experience and iterated insistence, and also about changing relationships over time and to time. That is, by beginning again, by constructing a fold or crease or pleat across the work, I was making all the poems as arranged vertically in a column somehow touch other parallel poems. The deep feelings of the fold, as well as related structures of evocative diagonal links (these are the Drafts using Roman numerals) and many kinds of random repetition establish the utopian possibility that all parts of the work are involved with all other parts. Each potentially touches on all. This is a topography of mutuality, of mutual pleasure and relatedness and an ecology of interrelated factors. I don't want to emphasize too exclusively that this could be (in post-structuralist terms) a "feminine" strategy; that idea is extremely charming (not to say theoretically prepared for), but even it does limit

[7]

things. It is more an erotic strategy or set of energies—let me say it that way.

That is how both the fold and the grid (something topological/ organic and something more geometric and mechanical) became structural and aesthetic principles of repetition, proposing relationships among the works. Looking down the grid of 19 x 6, the poems make a simple list or series through time (the time of reading, the time of writing); reading across the grid, one sees pleats and crimps of similarities across "lines" (my name for the horizontal group of six).

Reusing phrases and important (or just curious) images and lines from my own odd specific trope repertoire is, in a sense, randomly generated and as randomly "stopped" at number 19 to swing around again. Thus, for a kind of efficiency and a deeper undercurrent of potentiality, poems connect more or less, across a "line" that would be every 19th poem (say, poems 17, 36, 55, 74, 93 and 112). This solution also just happened and was accepted, although in fact anything can appear and reappear anywhere in the poem, making and participating in a texture of potential connections. One image of the task, as I've said, was "I am trying to write the same poem—the Poem—all these are just 'drafts' of that poem." But I really do know there is no capital P poem nor any capital B book. This rather sublime ideal (one Poem) allowed me to claim that I've got a couple of tries to write some poem in a particular place. But that place, it turned out, is not simply six chances on any given "line." It is 114 (plus) chances. And thus the universe is laughing, "poetry" thru the ages is laughing, I too am laughing.

"Thus one enters one's own life as a traveler." "Draft 94: Mail Art," page titled "R EST LESS," *The Collage Poems of Drafts*, 2011, 19.

~

Whether and how gender matters to a work like this—whether and how social location matters (social class, religious culture, national language privilege)—is something that, as a critic, would concern me. As a poet, I am first inside the language, inside rhythms and desires—including the desire for this poem and for any section of it—and then inside the history of poetry (including the long poem), which, I am aware, has (has had? is this in the past?) some very peculiar relationships to female practitioners. Social location and formal elements are both two separate things and, with many saturations and filiations, the same thing. Women writers are in a somewhat precarious, somewhat oblique, always fascinating cultural position. The ideologies and assumptions around gender power and expression are worth the study of a lifetime—the historical twists and turns of this aspect of culture have certainly engaged me. Gender can be a disadvantage, a vantage, and an advantage. It is like hands of cards one is dealt in an ongoing "game" of high seriousness, something engaging and demanding, and with real stakes. The struggles to achieve the possibility of some apt education, some liberty of expression, some cultural presence, some use of one's individual and collective powers are also engaging and demanding. This is not a tendentious statement, but a real feeling. And sometimes, from one's subject position, one faces the art products of the past with both admiration and resistance. So I have. In *Drafts* as a whole, struggling with culture until it allows for, is open to multiple otherness is a key goal; critique of great poems that are not yet adequately female-ized (or made even queerer still) is another response. Both are tasks I have repeatedly undertaken in this work.

I don't want to say too much about scale and gender, because any stereotypical observation—however situationally true—risks restating (re-instantiating) patterns we want to reject. I would simply say that our cultures need, finally, to treat differences in a non-binarist manner. This is a utopian goal. There are many ways in which it would be appropriate to claim that *Drafts* has a feminist implication; its author has a decentered relationship to general culture, even despite her cultural privileges. The work does negotiate the patrilineal—as most work by women implicitly has to, as we are still culturally uneven in full claims. The torquing that I do most often addresses male-authored works, but even to say this is overly limited. I am quite interested in anti-masculinist stances (these of course can be held by males), but not ones that deny authority. Authority without hierarchy would be a good motto. That's also a picture of the grid.

So Je est un Author: like Dante, Pound, Oppen, Coleridge, Wordsworth, Pope, Mallarmé, Virgil—figures I have addressed in *Drafts* as a whole. But there is a difference. Je est that other kind of autre/ other/ author as a conceptual act of disturbance and cultural recalibration. I am them as female author, which, speaking traditionally, is only a simulacrum of authorship throughout history. In the story, that is, in the particular story that literary history has often told, I am virtually non-existent, or unwritten, or only vaguely remembered, frozen out of whatever culture is hegemonic; then I am inauthentic, a pretender, a fake; somewhere in there I become ghost, revenant, plagiarist, copyist, chameleon, never doing things as well as those male others, haunting the other side of the world. Finally only in the last two or three centuries do I become (somewhat, sometimes) real. For now, even now, that history is marked by the shadow of me and of others like me. I am a female writer with a set of interlocking differentials of position and access, differing potential for dissemination and reception, if not in production. (Differing does not necessarily mean hierarchically organized along the lines of gender power—but it mainly has.) I am a particular writer—privileged in language and semi-privileged in country of national origin, critical in politics, invested in secular practices, via deeply rooted skepticism. I am this mix of hegemonic and emergent in relation to even the critical edges of that culture in which I am also saturated, and through which I have expressed my longing. Or part of that longing. Through which I have also expressed and exposed my resistance.

~

For me a poetics is expressed philosophically via the detail, but also in praxis—in titles, in formal ideas or visualizations of a possible page, of a possible work. This offers some sense of what is to be given when the poem or form is realized. What was, for instance, implied in the grid, as it "developed" like a photograph from paper exposed to light? In cruising thru old notebooks once, I found the generative page dated 4 November 1993—where I decide for the tactic of the fold and for the number 114. In that same memorandum to myself, I considered establishing a periodicity of 20, but thought it was boring, and noted that "pivoting on 19 is much more interesting," for, I said then, "no reason but the pleasures of arrangement"! I didn't then know about the Metonic cycle, pivoting at 19 years. I didn't even understand the interest and mysteries of prime numbers (19 is one), nor the fact that, with 19 as the periodicity, odd and even would alternate: that is, one set of poems would be "odd" (say Drafts 77–95) and one set of poems would be "even" (say Drafts 96–114). I am not a mathematician; I was just lucky.

I grew into my conceptualizations as they developed and then, as they were generative, I stuck with them as a loose plan. Who is to say why there were only "19" poems—why that number got so invested with oddity and numenosity. Why did the turn happen in 1993—seven years after beginning? Who is to say that 6 times 19 would be enough, that it would "give the idea of"—everything. (And also, as I have elsewhere proposed, that number would both address Ezra Pound's number of *Cantos*—127 et seq.— and let his number alone.) No one. Only myself, carrying out the charge (it was electrical) that the poem-as-my-ideas-of-it entrusted to me. A gift. A promise. That is, this work was always a promise—I am not writing book reviewer-ese here ("such a promising work . . . "). I wrote it invested always in my promise to it.

≈

It is no mystery to me why Draft 1 was called It, Draft 2 was called She and Draft 3 was called Of. The poem as a whole argues for what I'd call, in my own shorthand, the ethical acknowledgement of "of"—the of-ness indicated as relationality, intersubjectivity, betweenness. The poem certainly wants to talk of the mysteries of "it." And "she" is faced with that "it" and with all of it.

∼

Long poems, of course, have several pulses of ending, endings before the end. This seems to be typical of—a rule for?—the long poems of long modernity. There is never one ending. Endings pulse as much as any other part of a long text. By making the Précis, one might say I ended this poem halfway through, a long time ago compared with where the poem is now. There is also, in this particular book, "Draft 113: Index." And "Draft 107: Meant to say." And "Draft 104: The Book." And "Draft 100: Gap." Do you see what I mean?

∼

As one grows and changes, one's influences grow and change, and one mellows (somewhat) into the "tensuous" relationship one has with other poets. Why the neologism? Because these relationships are tense, tenso-like, and sensuous at once. And finally, one begins to understand . . . something. Some of the vectors. Or if not to understand, then to accept that these became the building blocks, and those the tools. For example, I was stunned by Robert Duncan's prose, particularly *The H.D. Book*, as well as by certain striking poems (like "Poem beginning with a Line by Pindar"). His unfurling of endless commentary and renegotiating with the past and with all he had said before presented midrashic lessons. Also Duncan gave lessons in passion, memory and invention. This means, of course, that I was also struck by H.D.'s prose. Their pensive, ode-like essays helped open one path to my long poem, long ago.

[12]

Duncan also is a struggling-hero of the heuristic (as in their own ways are George Oppen and Charles Olson, Robert Creeley and Robin Blaser, as well as others who are contemporaries in the long poem: Beverly Dahlen, Nathaniel Mackey, Alice Notley, Ron Silliman, Anne Waldman). The heuristic played for me as I figured out the various deep-structuring formal elements of Drafts as I was writing the poems. Each move was tested as a commitment. And a risk. And sometimes in despair. In the *Jacket2* section of commentary on *Drafts*, (from 2011), a number of people spoke about the crossed-out poem, "Draft 68: Threshold." This work was done in utter desperation. It was slashingly compelled by disgust and revulsion. Mainly to politics and to our time. and to my own place.

Thus it was not a gimmick. It was as much a shock to me as to anyone that the poem was almost effaced.

~

Among the various things one could say about it, *Drafts* is certainly a work saturated in an objectivist ethos. I picked up the thread of this poetics in my personal bond with Oppen (whom I first met in 1965), deeply affected by his intense poetic and existential engagements. When I began *Drafts* in 1986, Oppen's oeuvre and his example were very forcefully in front of me. He had just died in 1984. I had been working on the edition of his *Selected Letters* since about 1980, entrusted with this task by George and Mary Oppen at my request; that book was published in 1990. At that same time, in 1986, when I began *Drafts*, I had not read Zukofsky in any serious way. I was simply not yet engaged with the challenges of his oeuvre. Therefore the following dream event astonished me, this from a poem completed in early 1988: "Draft 6: Midrush." Midrush was my nonce word meaning the rushing around one experiences in midlife. That word, incidentally, was soon revealed as a crypt word for my secular version of midrash, and it prefigures the role that the genre midrash was to play in this work.

[13]

> Wraithes of poets, Oppen and oddly
> > Zukofsky
> > renew their open engagement with me
> > wreathing smoke-veils
> > my eyescreen tearing their insistent
> > opaque, startled
> > writing . . .
> > > (DuPlessis 2001, 35)

Drafts is certainly and not innocently drawing on Objectivist poetics. Indeed, here it appears to be haunted by objectivist poets.

The shock of the word "oddly" is that in 1987–88, I had, as I've just said, no evident poetic engagement with Zukofsky. However, about my early poem "Crowbar," someone had remarked that it seemed to be really influenced by Zukofsky, probably because of its cultural allusiveness, hermeticism (the title puns on "trobar"), and quickness of sound. I thereupon quipped—"Better to be influenced by somebody you haven't read than by somebody you have." Which is both amusing and self-defensive. The real lesson is—if you are influenced by someone whom you haven't read, you had best go and read this person. So I did. I found that in certain elements—notably the quirky generic range, the play of self-difference and sameness, and the subjective encyclopedism of the "cantos" I was writing, and the attenuations of secular Judaism—I had some things in common with Zukofsky's long poem. At the same time, in diction and sense of the line, as well as a general orientation to the serial and struggles with the socio-political, I had some things in common with Oppen's work.

> Yet no masters.
> Only practices can be adequate.
> > Only Citizenship
> > in languages.

∽

No poem is totally the poem you meant to write, but every poem you've written is the one you did or could write, brought to the poise or level of interest to which you could then bring it. That is, the poem escapes the poem. Or the poem escapes the poet. Or is it, the poem escapes the poetics? With the simultaneity of making and a sense of loss, something escapes inside the work. This "escape" authenticates the work.

〜

Every one of these "last" nineteen poems in *Surge* is in a double mode: each has some aspect of doubleness—a gloss, a commentary, substitute words, italic shadows. This expresses my reluctance to "fold up" an endless poem, a poem that is not (really) going to finish. Or to indicate that it does not fully complete itself in this book.

> This is however the situation
> of all poems
> in a set called poetry.
> There is no "a poem." There are
> only practices of making, of poesis.

> In a novel something must happen.
> In a long poem nothing
> happens? No, it's the whole poem
> that happens.

〜

What happens to the reader? I can only speak for myself, although I have a double role—writing these poems and reading them. But I think reverie/ aroused meditation is what certain interesting poems create. A reader feels the thinking as feeling. Duncan said something parallel in his 1979 lecture on Olson (published in the Lost and Found series): "[poetry] makes us feel presences because typically it follows a rhythm. . . . [giving] a feeling of a measure and a measure that's different from speech and creates what Aristotle found in Parmenides—a sort of hypnagogic state—so he disqualified it as philosophy" (p. 19). You are only half reading any work as such. You are in an echo chamber of you and it, your memory, its findings, your world, its elaborations, your blockages, its penetrations. Its words, its statements, its being, your various desires for it or resistances to it compel an intersubjective relationship between the poem and the you. You don't "create" the work (that is only one half of the intersubjective bond). It helps to create you, as you are confronted with making something of it. The dialogue can be intense, generative and metamorphic. (It can also be boring and a dud.) The extreme strangeness of reading is constituted by your private relationship with a public document made in words that we mainly can parse or define.

But that strange thought accounts for the deep function of poetic rhythm and sound and structures. Deep and inexplicable. These—the poem, its sounds—somewhat tune you—the work timbres you, it vibrates you ("tune"—bringing to the same tone is only part of the panoply of forces). The poem is almost limbic in its appeal, "rolled round in earth's diurnal course . . ."

∾

There is always a sense of social array in a long poem. There are always verbal triggers of "social evaluation" (as M.M Bakhtin and P.N. Medvedev used this term) in even small word choices (and this, of course, also in shorter poems). Working inside language is working inside a medium that everyone uses every day. It is a far different escapade than working in, say, ceramics, for people mainly don't know how to work clay. Our medium is where everyone is, what everyone uses. This is the most tremendous fact about and challenge of writing.

~

To what degree do historical/political events get registered and accounted for inside the poem? Some of this "social evaluation" occurs in language nuances, some in explicit references and allusions. Some via structures (line break, trajectories, the arc of parts and whole). Some because multiple-singularity (subjectivity) and numerousness are in constant dialogue in a text. And finally, in this difficult historical period of writing, I have begun to understand that my feelings are socially saturated—I draw on "political" feelings. I mean they are felt personally, subjectively, inside me, almost lonely at times—but they are political feelings. Real feelings—not borrowed, not tendentious, not defined by others or by groups. I feel, as Theodor Adorno once said, "migrated into" by our current realities, infused in every cell by an on-going world crisis of global plunder, ecological shocks, economic depredation, gender wrongs, and nationalist malfeasance. The political world infuses everything we are. I express it continuously; I do not have to "decide" to write a "political" poem—I write politically simply by trying to represent all the dimensions of my and our lives. The social world, the economic world, the political world, the gendered world are here, now. The question is how to face them, not to exclude their force by means of the purificatory or aestheticizing rituals of art.

~

These works are symphonic and have lots of moving parts individually and as group (as a "whole"). The poems as a whole try hard to resist poetry ideology. I am not that interested in poetry as the nicely tuned lyric (it's more the analytic lyric that is interesting), but, as it turns out, I don't resist either lyricism or passion. Sound and its enormous pleasures, syntax and its tricky pleasures are central to what I am doing, as is a quest for cultural resonance. These works also manifest a collage sensibility with edges and juxtaposi-

[17]

tions. I am fascinated by genres, including, as I mentioned, a root genre treated in a secular spirit: midrash. This means continuous gloss and re-gloss, evocation, self-citation, re-interpretation. These poems usually have notes—something quite a-normative for poems (though done by Marianne Moore, T.S. Eliot, Melvin Tolson, and some contemporaries). With this tactic, I risked seeming punctilious and academic (or at least scholarly) when all I wanted was to acknowledge the work, suggestiveness and formulations made by other people. Notes acknowledge the work of others—this is both a simple ethics, and a social gesture stating that any work's solidity is constructed of its cultural porousness, its willingness to enter into a network of contested meanings, its surface—is this another contradiction?—of depths.

∽

Time (writing time? reading time?) is the record of a multiple-singularity making its wayward, eccentric path thru plethora. This makes networks that exceed any closure that can be expressed. That's why closure is mooted.

∽

This poem will be smashed, lost, cited and absorbed.
  This poem will be stuffed in attic bookcases (the Lily Briscoe syndrome).

∽

Robert Duncan:
"The Master of Rime told me, You must learn to lose heart."
        Structure of Rime XX (*Roots and Branches*, 170)

[18]

Cy Twombley on his work:
"It does not illustrate. It is the sensation of its own realization."
   (from his *NYTimes* obituary in July 2011)

Surge: Drafts 96–114

Draft 96: Velocity

Pulses uneven, pushes
  surging air gusts, gusts plunge
   horizontally, sweeping
wings, its wings
  open and shut, balancing
   the swallowtail
gripping down.
  It snorkels precariously,
   fast as it can.

But losing the book with a Keats poem
  when we were in rough cut, and I had to teach
   "bright star" when we hadn't
processed the loss,
  blew me away.
   That this is a well-known dream-genre—
no consolation.
  Yet oddly witty.

Recklessness of life inside its own
  endangeredness,
   cross-hatched blasts of wind on wing—
it all came so fast
  one couldn't register it,
   except as ripped.
What is, is.
  What's torn is all.
   No readiness for the call.

What then went
  a-wander, shadowy
   over persons, apples, wall?

The discovery will be palpable, balancing
unsteadily on something impalpable.

All things, their else and verge,
their costs and lines of provenance,

be stark in the world in which
all that heart-breaking brightness will

crack. Day by day, I resist mourning
and yet it catches, wrenches, twists and

trips me—trips me!—I fall into it
"no place remaining" *Denn Bleiben ist*

nirgends and stand nowhere, though
temporarily here, ride and riven through,

tight astride the no of Yes,
inside a stranger, starker yes of No.

2. REMARKS

That gust of pulsing, wide and fast *plunging crosswise* push and change
that *made this mark, this / this \ like any brightness blown, any wing or leaf,*
I wanted to say it was *Parnassius mnemosyne* (clouded Apollo) *for its*
fancier name –which wasn't true. It was just a swallowtail in which the
word "memory" did not appear nor the touch of "poetry." *It was* just
ordinary, not endangered, no more than any thing.

Blustered with cross-drafts it holds tight. Creamy yellow, black lines and
marks *like letters on a page, shimmered in the wind and light* and ribbon-
wings with bright thought-dots, blue jot, red spot, rainbow quipu-

eyes. *I kept losing my place in the book* it hinged open and closed, *as if the letters, touching, read the word, the word the text.* Gripping down, it snorkels sweetness precariously, in transit.

But losing the book with a Keats sonnet *a painful sign* when we were in rough cut, and I had to teach *such statements of looming as* "bright star would I were" when we hadn't begun to process this loss—it blew me away. *Writing is impossible, reading is sadness, a word or sentence into void. It all could be summarized as "aftermath."* This well-known dream-genre is well-attested. Yet little consolation.

The recklessness of life inside itself, *the doubled turn of throws, of throes of fate* the cross-hatches of bluster, *the too-steep roads* the energy in wind and wing—all were *intercut* so fast one hadn't time to register this (any) time, except as ripped. What is, is. What's torn is all. *"We're coming here with pieces of people we lost." They are shadows tangled in the long vigil of the page.*

There was no readiness for the call. This "it" emerged almost unseen, lurking *films gray with scrims of untrackable –isms* shadowed under persons, apples, wall. *Under fold, under the scratched ink of palimpsest,* and under those tricky transcode systems *setting numbers to letters, then* words to those sums— *that pyramid of A becomes zero. Now read the newborn letter—is it from a stranger?* A stranger universe.

It will be palpable, yet balancing *who knew how* on something impalpable. *This really is a documentary.* All things, their else and verge, their costs and lots and lines of provenance, *the N's and Y's and Xing place and R's* stark in the world in which all that heart-breaking brightness will

break again. Day by day. I say I resist mourning *this mass of mixed hungers and desperate outcomes* and yet it catches, wrenches, twists and trips me—trips me!—I fall into "no place remaining" *Denn Bleiben ist nirgends*— What? Simply to BE is not in being rooted, but be blown away, be riding, riven   *further out than loss*

tight astride the no of Yes,
the no of Yes that shadows thought
inside a stranger, starker yes of No.
The yes of No that calls outright to A
no matter whether A is there or not.

January–February 2009

Draft 97: Rubrics

If
the red streak of honey in the mouth
If that rush,
fathoming up in fullness,

if the welling of sound, the englobed
honey-hold
thickens, resistant
        to flow yet flowing,
       despite we are in time
               whose henna dark touch
          smears us with plenitude and echo;

If there is speaking song,
              Multiple exposure to the bright debris
enters it
       rose-fish fish-rose faint in the tent of yellow smear
            opens to it, the day will,
       the light will, be striking it;

             THEN in the sweetness of the place,
THIS be Honey trying to speak.
       And riddle by riddle, notch to notch, petal and pollen
bright words WILL fall, twisting and drizzling,
           a-gleam with orange emanation (erudition) (elision)
and scattered into a red-gold light.

Red circled holes   Red rover red   Red squares
on cardboard   rover stepped   corner to corner
for stitching.   under and over.   supremacist principles.

This first page is a primer
       letters in orange blossom honey,

TRACE   suck them
clean from the finger. The house, the bee, the river, the door.
                                RED OCHRE
                words to be read, yet blurred,
smeared on the ghostly page, WORDS
muddied with clay, scraped with road rock
                                code letters of a security check.

        The paper informed me "you are at a crossroads"
        and then blew away, down the valley where the wind goes
gusting and twisting. Clouds, rose heart, straight to the airport,
                Rotting leaves. Take-off. Ear pressure.
All this could,
                with steaming lumps of compost
                outline time.
This letter is life, iota iota   humus humming   it is an encyclopedi
luminous in every gray-brown account.
        Luminous even in the depths of the newspaper.

        Spike password twist: what will allow MORE?
What will honor
        dialectical (diacritical) (diasporic)
resonance. Make the sign.
            A RAYED-OUT ROSE
Have you accepted?
        To sound each overtone petal while
            swirling, davening, loosened
                so far beyond vagaries of
                    suspicion as were willingly indentured
on selvedge and borderland, willing
    to work by the pollen light of day
    and watch the teardrop planet
            golden in the night
                druped above

a sprawling blue florescence.

This flickering little
yellow powder, dot and grain,
IS TRANSFORMED.
The world hangs here, honey off a spoon, a drizzled
thread. The brightness twists in lines—and then it falls.

Blood oranges, their marble paper peel—
THIS LIST of things, this next least
globule of cellular joy
is enough to stop one dead. Dead!

IT IS ALL RUBRIC,
given all is red.

Writing

on rainbow

ribbon

a black rosette

for garland.

A to Z

stenciled bloopy

N mountains

and Y mindful

fishing.

Brick edges

edged brick

mortared

at angles for

triangle friezes.

Make the sign.
Signs from impingement (impediment) (implosion).
                And the cardinal sang in the redbud tree.
Who could
believe that
this would happen but it did, RED pip PIP, piercing suffusions of magenta.

Not without vertigo, not without the vertiginous,
not without antic radicalism. It reverberated color as sound.
The gong struck at every step, A black O blue, desire Violet.
                        YELLOW STAIN

[29]

POOL OF PINK
always layers of matter, the matted mast of alphabet
rotting and steaming, filled with red-tipped worm

O dizzy dizziness, there's no rest here;
At the HEART
of the delectable comes floating. At a border
of the debatable comes zoning. At delight,
whitening mists for turns of anxiousness—
the blur of a car: is this the road? is this the moment? Is this poisonous
is this the premise (the promise) (the prefix)
so broken and yet still marked by streaks of light?

Where is this and what are we?

Beaded angel
pluck-dark
in-blood sound.
The hoopoes
came back year
after year, here.

Turquoise
chalice with
lotus narrative.
The butterfly
papyrus-color
landed on her lapis.

Vegetable harp
green shadow
wingly. Cloud-berr
yellow, memory
alembic. Rosy ribb
remember-red.

Secret crypts within the colors
dust us with the force of color.

Amber is honey reversed.
Attention!
There was a line of coral, a puncture of
BLOOD as, from a needle where was stuck
that fingertip, and then suck, taking your swift blood
or the blood of a hurt child into
your mouth.

Such astonishment seeing TIME move and bleed
into such a tiny pinprick of the universe,
        as temporality hit matter
and set us —smash and shatter—
                upon the wanton ground of our own wonder.

JANUARY–MARCH 2009

Draft 98: Canzone

After the experiences spoken of already, after I found that the luminous bit of phosphorescence in the dark room was a bug, pulsing blue, I wanted to show how these data are vectored. Yet even the lyric may trip and fall unwitting into brambles. Do I need again to prove myself vertiginous? I now open the book backward, as if shifting poles, and pass into a mirroring account of alphabets. Every off chance is the index of what has already been articulated, opening onto the same scrubby field. The master poet trembled. People watched him and wondered. He could barely articulate one shuddering, shattered word, but struggled, shaking, and thereby achieved exactitude and bearing. As for me, years later, I stumbled through a cracked gate, scarcely knowing why and how I was brought to this place. Its ownership in fact was common property, though at first it had seemed fenced off—*Vietato l'ingresso.* People watched me and shrugged. However, having finally come here, to an open book, I thought it plausible to write of the intersections, so that others might recognize their fate in mine as well as mine in theirs. Hence I composed a canzone that begins "I carried my soul the other night."

> I carried my soul the other night, I was
> angry at it and concerned and it
> was my own girl child who became
> smaller and smaller, not grown up
> into her own real self but small,
> a doll of dolls of dolls
> with the skin of a baby. Not
> a baby but someone looking
> near to six or seven, yet the size
> and shape of someone whom
> a mother could still carry, curled and nestled,
> a cozy infant of about eight months
> which is why I called this my soul.
> And I spoke to her that night and through the day.

Two barrettes and a scrunchy were at issue
the way it's always something simple,
a pretext for feelings too large to speak of,
yet when I remembered this insight, it was
way past the event, thus coming far after I
had needed the helpful decoding to
what this then had meant, and therefore felt
confusion, bitterness and curiosity: why
did you not tell me you needed them
to swim. Or to be on the team
for soccer, or whatever, everything
traveling backwards and behind-hand.
Was it too late now to buy or find those
pretty clasps and bands to give my soul?

Why didn't you tell me what you needed
from the beginning? I wanted everything
to give us satisfactions and
connections. What could have occurred
between us? Instead there were silences,
repressions and symbolic sniping gestures.
Yet when I carried you, you nestled
the way they do, and milky soft
against me and you carried me, I
looked precisely like you, or you looked
like you, those lively eyes and dark curls
and spunky disposition and I was moved and
critical, was I any good a mother? I had thought
I was a better mother, she a soul.

"You will have," I was told or said, "to share
the guest room, as a crowd of people
is already there," and I lay her down to rest with them.
"There are dancers and readers and those who

would not be satisfied, and there you will go to school,
a clandestine girls' school, and with you are
people you once knew and some are dead.
Attend them through the many tales and songs
that each might offer others or invent.
The room is small, so work it out.
They will wait for you as you for them
with yes and no, with back and forth,
the here and there, the then and now,
their modes of folding and their modes of caring."

I was struck by this lightning
as much as she, and I carried
the soup quietly to all the beds, for all
through the house it was dark, as it would have
had to be, and darker the movement
stair to stair. There were many there to feed.
We must all feed all the living, then the dead.
And I, it seemed, had taken on one task. Don't spill it.
"I won't." A vow. Was I alone? I did not seem to be
though this was hard to fathom when I felt
the red shadow of our bloody world's
insistent presence in the moon's eclipse,
darkening night. And then the moon slid
slowly back with full suffusing light.

Yet this part of the work remains closest to darkness.
The knowledge of yearning will not be complete.
There is no there; it's all degrees of here.
Cannot touch them whom we are marked by.
But they are palpable and enter this place.
Be nomadic, nomad. Wander with the wanderers,
yet safe in the room. There is at once too much
and much too little. Wait it out.

[34]

"The bit of ugly, the glitch, the torn, the sweeper, the tender,
the constant reminder that things are being made, unmade
and tended" —you are now one part of all of this.
You will be it, help it, answer and feed that
surface of cries, chirps. You will call out.
Live in empathy. Let the agony be. Comfort it.

Reject the whole that someone claims is rule.
A hole, a line, a hold, a lie, a hope,
a hype will slide you through this most dangerous spot.
Resist only rectitudes, resist the crazed
and driven knowers. Find and replace.
Though the mechanism to depict this is
called documentary, still it needs the stinging
pulse of lines. This matches that.
All "of-ness" exists
for much more Of.
The beyond moves to two places: here and there.
To achieve connection,
is there just one route of passage?
There is not.

This canzone is divided. What is the method in such a song? How was
the evidence for this police report assembled? The first part is the
first, and the way it begins is repeated variably—"I carried my soul."
This is insistent. The second part is the second, and very short—there
is no particular need for balance except as this part pivots between
two units of three each—and begins "You will have . . . to share."
The third fissions and fissures ("I was struck by this lightning") so
that it becomes impossible to follow and, as was already intimated,
gets caught in its own cross-hatches and brambles. These divisions
offer quixotic gestures at best, hardly a tribute to my powers of
construction, but rather to my sense of being overwhelmed. For
saturation in the material is so great that to speak of controlling this

experience, or of dividing the representation presents no more than a temporary artifice or stay against the world as such. Truly to say what is here still to be said, I would have to divide, but also to multiply the poem again and again, aphorism after aphorism. What is its argument anyway? When this canzone became known—was there a backstory to this? was I ever in the anthologies?— a friend asked me what my definition of OF was.

We are still working without a contract. There is a continuous, often weaseling use of the word "challenge" whenever policy is being discussed. Tying up tomatoes is on my list for today. She still has the tattoos from where her head was held *en pointe* for the radiation beam to be directed. I fear continually that I will not finish what I define as "my work," so I keep adding other tasks and possibilities, doubling already doubled poems, for example, which is, to speak perfectly frankly, an obvious and transparent strategy. If you start "deepening content knowledge in reading," you might end up reading between the lines. Then between those and other, secret lines. I would like to give you this small piece of string.

Afterward, I could perhaps write interstitial poem after poem, filling gaps that have opened and that exist (have in fact always existed) between every single word, obliterating the work until it is one over-written, unreadable, but theoretically conceptual and thus critically consumable textual object whose laws and rules have, over time, become superstructure. Or I could refuse to. Afterward, I could begin again backwards, moving from the end to the beginning. "Awful literal these words." And many others. Act as if you felt the lines of force, the connections. Act *because* you felt them. Rescue children—even if there is no guarantee. Of their future. Of anything. The person is a pinhole through which the whole community beams and takes itself into its own arms, *camera oscura* images projected, dancingly, upside down; their melancholy, their intersections, their humor, their charm, all cross and link, but sometimes don't. Vita nuova. We hold each other and apart. This part commences here.

June–July 2009

Draft 99: Intransitive

It's not just the dead   are coming closer   it's
    that their smiles   their jutting silvery eyes
██████   ████
    a rasp or clasp of voice   become intransitive.
    And then   as cellular touches   flashes
  broken and re-mended   remanded
bone fibers   are, are not.   ███████████ we entwine
    with these lengths
of marrow,
    with unimaginable lost ██████ intransigent
with ████ no ████ with them   not   the pointing ████████.

    A golden intention   *Diverge!*   *Receive!*
motivated this   tracking shot   yet
    the camera leaky   █████████████
the old stock too fast for humid gray   luminosity   for the
████ pale light   on the pines.

It's not just the dead
are coming but to run to sleep to travel to wonder to die
    are hypotenuse announcements
of a literal vector.   ████████ crosses metaphoric space.
  It's not just
    solidity of claim   v.   dissolving with an intermittent mark.
It's their   floating   across. But   where to   where?

    So band of odd light   cross't green fuzz   furze
  so pollen stuck in the throat
vvvvvvvvv who sees   what   projection   coming across or not –
you need the dead   closer   but not ████████████
    Compromised these
findings.

    This marks the urge to put everything in. This is it

████████████. This is the Book. X upon X   overwritten
        wanting to say everything ████████████ dark
                matter filling space.

The complete   is never complete.
"Everything   in it   is both head and tail   alternately   reciprocally"
        And listen—   What's out there?   Opalescence?   Opacity?
It is the dead,
and coming closer.
Silvery   like the
Moon in all 4 corners of the page   shedding tricky watermarks,   and they
declare themselves
from phase to phase.   In dark phases   more oddities
seeds or stars   are pressed in the paper.

Figure of
who or which   stripped in any ████████, █
        walk thru the daily,
a black compost where we stand, rotting   generative   in transit.
In
is the effect   fecund   on the spongy needles   as the hikers
tread the up-built bounce of pine.
It's literally   all we have to go on.

The dead are coming closer   and those   who walk this
raggedy line   are ████████████.   This predicament
        "alternately and reciprocally"   ████████████.
        ████████████ alit   then went.
So chartreuse warbler   lands and parts
                    Plus a tiny toad, too,   the opposite
            ████████████   ████████████

        Indicate! Envelop!
Saturate with   overtones   of echo.   You'll need to

[39]

██████████████████████ in the most dazzling cloud.
   Throb! Furnish! Consider! Avail! ████████████████████
    Bright streak
the echo there already,
    which watery call into the waxing wobble—
its *impalpable sustenance* ██████████.
   Wood thrush. That's what that was.   Like our robin, but hidden
Yet no riddle has an answer. Present imperative only.

██████████████████████ Such irony RE: years, suppose I put
2009. There. And now so what?
Remaining true for now. The date
creeps backward administering odd frissons inside the
inevitable   forward dock.

██

This says the dead are coming closer with their odd-shaped smiles.
My smile for theirs my lips on theirs we intertwine.
For we exchange a poet's kiss each other's eros to the side.

Three things collide—
now, then and after
the ends come loose, pitch down all streams
of the dialectical watershed it's here, there, and pooling
me you and many else tongue groove and slot
Is there anyone who is focusing this lens?
██████████████████. Refraction pov not quite a
fly's eye but noir zip and double closer
triple cross. The actor arranges coins in a grid
    we know this story, why tell this story?
    Alternatives insist on being marked, but dark.
  An unused room next door a room in use.
██████████████████ Secretive, this secret space.

The dead are coming.   Each room of itself
in that old time place
with an open side
fanned out to darkened watchers
and breathing worlds.
The coins go over the eyes
and in the mouth.
This text is made of traps.
The man is still there,
an old story of "gaper delay"
looks like
a frog, splash hard
on the white page
plunk
pen in his hand
poised glee
and utter irascibility!
Joy to see him   just like that.
"Come back," he said
"when you have learned the alphabet."

"I will."   A vow.   The letters fall.
        ▮▮▮▮▮▮▮▮▮▮
        What marks to put in the world
        and in what world?
        ▮▮▮▮▮▮▮▮   To inside it
    the you of me,   the me of it?
        ▮▮▮▮▮▮▮▮▮▮▮ hardly begins to cover it.
    So "In this section,   there is much crossing of hands."

18 is l'chaim, or life,   with its   180 degree rule,   so what's off sides?
is all the rest.
19
is when the project finds itself out

[41]

political, economic, quotidian, shallow,
rent, obnoxious, highlighted, ███████████████████████████
███████████████ "displays of mental confusions
with intrusions   of irrelevant information(s)."

                    19 is after life

Nor is it yet or particularly
death   but stands   in any place   as temporary
"center"   and pivots   round and round
then moves   its site   and tries again.   It is strangeness woven
in and out the strange, with the sprockets and cells
of estrangement   ███████████   and at home, yes, home,   but where?
in the world—yes, and   yet   which world
in the world?   analog belatedness?   digital freestyle?   you need to look out,
and see what the dead keep doing   after all.
There was a   kiss, a bit   a star   a clasp.
Indicate!   Keep!   Expand!
There was the cocoon swaddle   of all this music,   a seed sac
        in the body pod of chord
that splits;   and out comes ███████████   silvery and blue███
from the other side.   *Who knows but I am enjoying this?*
Even death? Well . . .   Bulge of wisdom   And intensification,   And curiosity.
Increase of alphabets.   Immersive lexicons.
Insatiate henceforward.

MAY–JUNE 20(

Draft 100: Gap

Dark landscape, its disordered order,
a walk shrinking into the mist.

Bright landscape, desperately
hot and dry and dusty. Both.

I leave places I've not yet got to,
and cannot then arrive at others.

And other ones again _____
_____.

Did these years have to happen
the way they did? _____

_____. The poem, unwritten
is concealed by the poem,

written. And in it.
There was always to be

another one. Beyond
_____.

There were the unseen,
the unheard, the unprojected,

unprotected. _____
_____.

As I read the sentence
"It is more arduous

to honor the memory

[43]

of the nameless

than that of the renowned,"
a door slammed in the corridor.

What's here is here.
But what is next

is not clear yet.
_____.

Hyper-scrite lecturer.
Quiet. Settle yourself.

_____. This is
a cross roads but nowhere

striking, and while there are
rocks marking the path,

they look no different
from the rocks all around anyway.

And did that path or the other
lead anywhere? _____?

_____? The other
side of words _____.

Can I remember what I was saying?
What did it amount to?

I assumed it mattered
but maybe there wasn't enough

silence. _____
down the fig-tree roadway

_____.

To spook the crows, someone

threw string-tied bottles
that will blow and glitter

over the seductive branches
fully laden, but as yet

only with hard, inedible figs.
One wanted to let them ripen.

_____.

How many words can hang from,

can depend on five trees,
fourteen-odd bottles

knocking their shiny plastic sides
together, in the wind?

_____

_____.

Try to be more than callow;
try to be more than curdled.

Slow down. The task
is luminosity. Darkness.

[45]

The complete
is never complete.

What implicates what?
What is necessary? What not?

You can see finally there are
two stories — _____

_____ and_____,
_____ but all diffused. Obscure.

Didn't I want, finally,
to write the second?

Never clear that I did.
This is a gap.

Or an opening. _____
_____,

the pattern unstable,
unstatable, extending itself.

_____.
_____?

Hunger for the next letter
makes the letters very difficult.

But if there were no hunger?
Then _____?

[46]

Can someone translate
the language of this work?

Guttering words, blown words,
light gleaming, yet distanced.

What is the truth
of the matter?

Let it go.
It is finished.

Even if it is not
complete?

Even if,
even that.

Will I not be lonely?
I am afraid to. Not to.

I am afraid so. This is

_____.

Be alone and quiet. Listen. There
will be a second other language.

The volta will happen
when the poem is over.

_____. _____
_____.

MARCH–MAY 2009

Draft 101: Puppet Opera

Perhaps make
a *hinge*
picture.
(folding yardstick, book. . . .)
develop
the *principle of the hinge*
in the displacements
1st in the plane 2nd in space

find an *automatic description*
    of the hinge

---

    perhaps introduce it
    in the hung/suspended woman

        Marcel Duchamp,
        Green Box.

Hung/suspended woman:
Why am I hung up here? What am I being hung from?

Another puppet, male:
It's not from. The text says, in "a hinge picture" or somehow in "an automatic description."

H/SW: I mean, not what the text says. But my situation.

AP, M: Why should I care about your situation?
This text is a plan for a work of art.

H/SW: A work of art can have alternative plans.
Care about my situation because it could happen to you.

AP, M: Unlikely. By definition. Totally.

H/SW: I am "LE pendu femelle." What definition is that?

AP, M: No ultimate ambiguity: you are hung/suspended as a thing. You are female animal thing. But I'll tell you, to me you look like a puppet of origami. Very compact. Angular. Folded very neatly. Immobilized with your own strings.

H/SW: The strings are mine? It that the whole of it?

AP, M: Well, I don't have strings. I work differently. Your strings don't belong to me. Plus, I'm not immobile.

H/SW: I can't tell much about you from where I am. But you should care about my situation because I could fall and hurt you.

AP, M: I will predict it. I will see it happening. I will move. Before you pitch down.

H/SW: Actually, all I want is know what the mechanism looks like to you. What's the machinery? How am I suspended and what am I hung from? I am too twisted up to see much.

AP, M: You seem to have clear plastic strings from the top. Almost invisible ones. But they seem to be closing your hinge. You are wrapped. Red shift, green afterimage. There is a large, solid structure above you. But in other lights, I can't see it. It doesn't come and go, but sometimes I can't see it.

H/SW: Are you different or the same?

AP, M: I've told you. My sense — my knowledge of myself — totally different. I am not suspended. I am grounded. I am on the plane. I am straight. I am mobile. Plus I have multiple fingers stiffening me underneath.

H/SW: What should I do?

AP, M: Why do anything? No one needs you to do anything. No one's asking you to do anything. You are in a good place, hovering folded up like that, tucked away, in space.

H/SW: I'm a bit uncomfortable; can't you see I am?

AP, M: When you talk about your discomfort, you're making me very ill at ease.

H/SW: I don't want to be immobilized. I don't want to be a trussed thing.

AP, M: There's no reason for that preference; it might just be a whim.

H/SW: I want to be straight and on the ground.

AP, M: Perhaps the very air is your ground. It's a lovely thought.

H/SW: You are only describing my hanging here with a metaphor.

AP, M: You are taking all this so literally; how can you be that unpoetic?

H/SW: I mean you are not telling me a physics or a mechanics but a justification.

AP, M: Well, you look nice up there. I like you can barely see the strings.

H/SW: This could be more serious than you know. Perhaps I am the Hanged.

AP, M: You are still talking. You are not Hanged; you are hung up.

H/SW: I don't understand the translation problem. No matter the name of this, it's off. What would happen if we changed our given names? Begin again. I'm tired of this.

"Pap po pap pup pip-ay,
here's a charm to another way."

AP, M: "'Pap po pap pup pip,' then.
Perhaps we can begin again."

Now you will be Pond-dew Fee-melle. I will be A. Larrey Dore.

Pond-dew: That's a change? Why are you giving me my name?

A. Dore: Don't you love that I love you? Don't you love that I adore you? Don't you love that I obsess over you? That I look up to you?

Pond-dew: When is adore not adore?

A. Dore: I know at least one door that's both A and not-A.

Pond-dew: Two contiguous doorframes, at a corner, one door, and hinges. Yet when one side is open, the other must be shut.

A. Dore: No, that's totally wrong. Though how can that matter even if it's true? It's such a piece of wit, so intelligent, so cunning, so—avant-garde. It changes everything.

Pond-dew: It's a particular case. But even changing all of art is not changing everything. Something is still not part of this critique.

A. Dore: One thing it does change—a categorical proverb: a door must always be open or shut. This door is neither and both. That is a change.

Pond-dew: Think about halfway there, for just a little air. That cunning door still goes tick and tock, like a clock; when your side is open, mine is shut. And the other way again, shifting advantage side to side.

A. Dore: You are too absolute. I just said it could be both. More complex. Besides, open is not necessarily advantage.

Pond-dew: Try being tied. That's what I have. That's where I am. That's what I think.

A. Dore: Isn't a Bride always tied? Isn't Ideal a damn good deal? Isn't a Vierge just poised on the verge? I envy you your place.

Pond-dew: I'm snarled up. Hung here and trussed. You'd see. There has to be some machinery not structured like this.

A. Dore: The door is witty; it's not like you describe. You can put the door at an angle so both sides are open.

Pond-dew: Why is this fact not true of me, then? Why is it true only of the door?
Time is up!

A. Dore: I think you are asking too much.

Pond-dew: Why can't a hinge picture work so we both go in and out? I crave a sense of mobility, of opening.

A. Dore: Do you want to be just like me? That's impossible. You are enough like me in being fee-male. You contain the male in fee. You hold him tight.

Pond-dew: No, not like you; like me.

A. Dore: What about pleasure?

Pond-dew: Whose? Is yours ours, is mine thine?

A. Dore: Nothing more can change, nothing in this situation can be more viable than what is here. We need eros, we need desire, we need yearning. And eros is difference. It is distance. It is having you exactly where and as you are. That's a syllogism.

Pond-dew: A Scylla gism. But you can imagine as much difference as you like; it's your fantasy. But when I am bound, I am up here for real.

A. Dore: I can't function without difference. It's unreal to think I can.

Pond-dew: I can't function so inhibited and held.

A.Dore: I'm sure you secretly like your bonds. Being tied. Maybe even erotic.

Pond-dew: My eros, your eros, and my civil status have to be disentwined. These strings cut. I am, so far, just my entanglement. I resent being immobile. I'm still twisted up here; all this talk, all this smart talk and nothing has changed. There is no rapture without rupture. I want to be down on the ground. I want to be fully open.

A.Dore: Even your impotent rage is erotic.

Pond-dew: Go off in a corner, then, and pretend you are a bachelor.

A. Dore: Cul de sac, cul de sac, cul de sac.

Pond-dew: Why must the erotic depend on the sex and the sexes that people imagined a hundred years ago? Do I show a little bit of ankle?

A. Dore: Fuck you.

Pond-dew: It was strange watching you. Peculiar. Isolated.

A.Dore: It was strange having you watch. Watch over. But I did come.

Pond-dew. Fine. And so could I, if I could untie my hands from where they are. But don't you think we should begin again, again?

A. Dore: I think we need another set of names. Just letters, sort of neutral. And no transformative charms and magic spells.

Pond-dew. I will be "H"; I like that cross-bar, holding equal things together. Or, maybe, apart.

A. Dore: I guess I'll keep "A."

H: We both have cross-bars.

A: We both have sexes, but sometimes you be "the" as he and sometimes I be only partly me. She? I don't know—some things I want I cannot tell. But might. From A thru H to ze?

H: Some things I want I cannot tell. Or won't. And so? We could we can we might begin to speak. We could, we can, we might mix all things up, redress the balance, do cross-over leaps. But I am still hung up right here. Why?

A: So let me actually take a look at what you are being hung from.

H: You said from the text.

A: A text is just a text. There are other issues, but I can't really bring them into focus.

H: I can't tell if this text is a suggestion or an authority. Anyway, what it's saying is: "find an automatic description of the hinge"

A: Automatic? Knee-jerk? I can give you whatever's in the dictionary. That's as automatic as I know. But it still is information. A how-to for this machine. "A jointed or flexible device permitting turning or pivoting of a part." If we changed, would the dictionary?

H: Go one step at a time. Flexible, turning. It depends; it is contingent. I think it's true about changing—words have histories but are not totally fixed. Why then am I fixed and bent and held?

A: A hinge goes only one way.

H: A room is only in one place—so they say. But in the realm where we now live, doors could swing further back and around. It depends. What are they used for, how imagined, what opening means.

A: Your function seems to be this function. To stay.

H: Perhaps for you. For me my "function" differs mightily. Has range and play.

A: So it's not just from the text, hung as if from the text, but the text is nonetheless here, justifying. Provoking. Riddling.

[55]

H: The definition says flexible; the situation is not. If I go by the definition, perhaps I'm not so fixed as it appears. I need to re-read this.

A: Are these structures real or did we imagine them?

H: Structures? Strictures? Isn't it a little of either and both?

A: Look at the real, look at the imaging consciousness, and look at their links. It's at least a triple-pronged task. In advance of itself.

H: That's the three-way allegory of the double door. It all hinges on that. And I do agree it's never only either/or. And I'm still where I was, but—

A: Maybe you aren't so fixed, it's true. Weird. The text confuses one thing with another.

H: So it does seem to be a mix: thinking and mechanics. Both have moveable parts, but both are being held. They are in sync for stasis, not for change.

A: Both need interpretation—the case is not open and shut, not easy to understand.

H: They need to be interrupted! If it is a mixture, interpretable, how come only I am being held?

A: Are you sure it's only you?

H: You were saying before, blah blah, that you could move freely.

A: Yes, I think I can. But it's not just me that's doing it. There's a question of agency . . . .

H: There's a question of leverage . . . . There's something odd about the leverage of a hinge. It is interior to the hinge and spread between.

A: Let me try to feel out the question of displacement. Hold it! It's become literal! My underneath is making me move.

H: Two sides linked together, fitted together with a pin, balanced, fixed but flexible.

A: I have been displaced! I was moved over here and now got totally stopped. I am stuck under you and suddenly fixed. Just where you could crash down! I don't understand my lack of will. Suppose you do fall—Now I could actually be in danger!

H: Do you want to understand it? What about will? What about fall? What about displacement? We are not so different. But I will try to fall (if I fall) so I don't hurt you.

A: I appreciate that. It's important that at least one of us survives to figure this out.

H: That's a useful sentiment—for you. I want survival too. But I never want to see others hurt. Or anyway, rarely.

A: That's a useful sentiment—for me. It is just so hard for me to stop banking on it.

H: And haven't we begun to figure it out? A hinge has two sides, both necessary. The pin holds and pivots. The hinge opens and closes. While some hinges are uneven, the ones that hold best are the same size, equal on both sides of the turn.

A: That's pious.

H: It's just mechanics. And it seems to be what works. We may move differently, but we then are both mobile insofar as we open a door. And a door is another kind of hinge. So is a book. Maybe this will work.

A: I think we need to work this out.

H: We are working it out. But I feel unhinged.

A: You are no longer bent. You are opening. Something's happening. You are sliding into the air very slowly and opening.

H: I am getting to the ground, on the same plane. I'm here. It's happened.

A: You have arrived at the ground.

H: No one is hurt. And we are both on this ground.

A: Now what? Now exactly what?

H: Let's see if we can investigate your Hand Underneath.

A: Could also follow where your Plastic Strings may lead.

H: Not to speak of analyzing the whole stage.

A: This whole stage. This whole machinery.

AUGUST–SEPTEMBER 2008; APRIL 2009; FEBRUARY 2010

Draft 102: One-on-One

Happy birthday, Contingency. Your troth
I bind and bid. I brood and bide.
      Mouth and eye,
      moth and cup,
"double fault with precarious vessels,"
earthly phosphorescence with its purposes
      a surtout of baggage
      in the garden of Muthe—
happened how? what just occurred?

Detraining I go back
      for her luggage (whose?)
      over drams with snow,
barriers with wire networks, where the strings and cold
      led through houses and families.
      I had to drag and dredge
remembering and forgetting,
beginning and losing,
backwards and forwards:
      even almost never when,
      and then
      whenever almost odd.

That leggy girl-self
coming vaguely into focus
      shakes unsteadily,
tripping on purling atoms of unevenness.
      So call her "her or me."

There was a second or third beside her
      wandering in cadence,
      a familiar cadence
      of familiar visitations,
with a hollow ring of bone about the bone.

One heard horse snuffles of a working family,
pulling, grazing, nuzzling, lumbering.
Saw Rachel of the longue durée
    she of the shadow poems
    writing a name for a day
    and writing of no name.
Saw a sweet dog peeing, anything
to wet and soften, as if in a dream.

What dramas did these characters propel
    what toil of tide
    what surge of fate,
what bespoke selvedge, what diva borderlands?

It was, maybe, simpler.
Someone here or there
took and claimed
an "idiosyncretismic weigh"
very much like this aspired to.

Handsome and tall as you, girl,
that other she was also,
he was, they were, and we,
new pronouns,
new others, further questioners.
And other further ones again . . .
"Parallel lurches,
what do you want
of me?" I said and thereupon

lurched with them,
stumbling each to ouch,
all into all,

us soon a-singing
from discrepant scores,
5 tunes, 4 meters, 3 keys, 2
full orchestras and 1 gold ring, mixolydian.

And other lurchers test the rocky site,
the moor, the furze, il campo, champs,
the itchy grass, the plain
or boggy seep, in short, whatever place
abutted up against

the apparently impassible
mountain range
that one began with.
History has no telos
it turns out. Just
various skirmishes:

make sure children do not die
of the preventable;
assure enough clean water,
nourishing snacks;
get everyone reasonably settled
here or along the way,
and consider whether it is wise
to kill.

Then, maybe, reading.

Even this was difficult enough
and kept on devolving.

So who among the lurchers found
that Crotch of Yes to catch,

the why that had been made
so tempting, hook of the world
the astonishing world
trawling softly through the stream
that never stops its flow.

Why does it matter who?
It's someone did.
More than one. And one again.

For this is another now, despite the plays
and travels already elaborated.
This clearly still unfolding, despite
magisterial stagings, this
still indeterminate.
Still ready.

Hypnogogic during all transitions,
hyper during the cacophonies and stompings
to which I lent
a wobbling mezzo and a wiggling foot,
I kept losing my exact place
around the rests.
But who cares?

Error is obviously
the muse of this;
not Eros, not Erato, but
error compounding error
venturesome
and ecstatic
on a backdrop of enormous
fullness

in which there is one small dot
(if you can find it)
that contains everything
possible to know (or so
it is poetic to declare)
but compacted into a single
explosive incipience.

Of working out
the postulated syntax of that dot
I/she/ we/they and you did speak.
Of being in this oddest world.
Of being a register of receptivity
and compulsion. Of passion.

These several fractalizing sets of
forces ended rapt together.
One-on-one on one or another,
the ark of one's life with mobile
pairs and clumps of this and that.

All sought to manifest fervor
by any hold that flesh and light
could twist;
all found that they were
two ends
of the same rope,
wrestling with awe
at what they touched.
Themselves

locked into, snarled up,
roused beyond by power and by
seeking it. Or seeking

to be overcome
by contact and by searing.
Or severing and yearning to be joined.
Or cut and torn
and marked by bone ripped
from the silvery dome of cartilage.

There'll be a song, a sprong, a nub or turn or twist
will serve as seed and pulse and thrust.
Neither dance nor sweet melodies
but only stun,
a burning one-on-one,
the pleasure
that happens hap, with ruthless happiness
as end and entering it.

AUGUST 2009, JANUARY 2010, JULY–AUGUST 2010

Draft 103: Punctum

1.

She being "trapped," she said, on a long ride to a faraway place, lights dim or are blown out, strain of the journey's not-quite endlessness, the bus is a shipping carton on wheels, the continental road fiercely straight. The woods on either side darken the bus, the pines hardly broken by flashes of light, a stolid endless unrolling zone of black-green. As the light changes, the pines change from shaggy to backdrop flat. This being a very long ride across much of the country, she doesn't want (always, or now, how did she say it?) to return to that version of home where she is implacably heading. Who does? Where is the zone of the long write, the ride as if in neutral, all anonymous travelers quietly napping, all the vulnerable laid bare, hats pulled down so no one can see in, and music humming into their plugged-up ears, as the silver-slushy bus goes down roads that all appear the same. A coolish dusk-hue dimming fast to fade. It was a long journey, yet perhaps not long enough.

Poetry
accentuates the void.
Should it soften it?   *How much stark is actually wanted?*
Words hang there (meaning here),
mite by matter, but by bit,
cannot by canto, etc.
                    Sentences inside sentences

I am interested
to represent time in words,   *awkwardly articulated.*
time's passage,
where a little swerve
translates what we have

[65]

into what we
(suddenly-abruptly) were.
This has been consistent
from Day One.

2.

Found in a thrift shop, old notebooks. Old date books, other peoples'
agendas, with former appointments scribbled in. A scrapbook with
pasted postcards. Where once someone had been. A there. Someone
had long ago used the give-aways from an old motel, thinly colored
rotogravures they were, to advertise where she or he had stayed,
to send this message to a friend, yet about 10 cards spliced and
extended in this notebook, so that the image itself was spliced and
extended, pasted down, elongated across a collaged page of repetitive
rectangles. Sliced up. Ruled down. Unsendable. Unique. Out here,
some one had been making something once, and here it is. Or was,
but

what artifacts less randomly
survive? That sounded
desperate fast. I didn't count
on feeling that.
Yet noting the collective
presence of absence
is not for everyone.

> It erases "the" specificity
> of each of us, anti-sentimentally;
> it over-generalizes,
> it even paralyzes.

> It is a flat black wall
> maybe with a few names.

[66]

3.

There is generally a lack of verbs, but not always. There is a discussion of verbs. Again, inconsistent. I looked out at the woods. One could get lost there, all too easily. It was a long walk, neither signposted nor very well blazed. What did I expect? The path is the one that a rich neighbor had cut further and with no particular insight, so with all her money, she blocked the spring, and water, finding its way as it will, has now undermined the path she thought she had controlled. Verb has to be thought through. Agency is all very well and good, power can be exercised, but then there is the land. Its forces. A lost specificity found. The ledger's incalculable underside declares itself.

On the small trail of the path
in the middle of the woods
of my time—well . . .
it all seemed reasonably familiar.
Suppose another world
where this was changed—
suppose I disappear.

4.

Tch tch
zt, zt,
Jetztzeit
width, length
bias, height.
And the tock part of the tick.

"The reader will find
that the categories
named 'trivial' and 'important'
are inextricably mixed."

I couldn't, once upon a
longish ago time,
tell any difference twixt
those "big hands"
second and minute.
Said to be simple— It wasn't.

Even in retrospect,
even now,
learning to "tell time"
remains difficult to do.

Tell it what?
For telling time has shifted to
the question of a so-called
"living hand"
piercing upward from
fast beneath the earth
stark beneath the page.

Nothing grand
here finally. A touching
smallness. Punctum.
The future of the past.

5.

The city sparrows zoom around this
corner now, their staging place
that new, well-growing pear.
We planted it.
We watered it.
We cared for it.

The detail
is a spiritual instrument.

6.

All of it (a suggestive rhetoric, untrue)
—the gesture, the space,
the boomerang throw,
the reflection a hundred times
over the piled layers of substantial bone once meat—
produces strange changes of scale.
In the staining there is coloring
in the draining is drawing
in the dripping is fraying.

There was a full body, cooked. Covered with brown gravy and a little
extra stew meat. In a big trencher, a flat trough, rectangular shallow
pan just long enough for a body, lying in brown meat gravy. Body
fully done, as brown as the gravy, just a bit eaten off or into already.
Nothing distinguishing—no face, but still this was a real body, lying
in gravy stewed with the stew meat. An antique body, a zombie
figure. Distinctive, but all changed. Unprepared, the little hungry
wanderer comes to here, to face this meat, through the ghost side
of the path. Should the hungry wanderer nibble it? She weighed the
options. A considered, if reluctant, finding (because she was quite

hungry)—eating this was too much. Too much like cannibalism. But not implausible. A choice. Thus one might eat or decide to eat, the avatar of one's own pure cooked meat.

7.

The words insisted on
  wily mourning, wily pleasure,
    verb! verb! verb! and combination!

Combin— looming. Intoxication.
  Storage in rectangles, shelved or splay and reach,
    dramatizing space behind, in back, beyond.

I dreamed I bought a dress (a dress? a me?)
  marked down forty-odd dollars off —
    $114 to 73.

What's meant by this? my poem? my life?
  Capricious and sibylline is spent
    such striking number-dredging night.

8.

There you are, you bees, homeless whirring clinging
to the face of the destroyed –the tree was rotten, but and yet perhaps
we can move the chunk of trunk for you
retain the hole wherein is hive
which now you know you hardly want
so changed it is from something that we do not understand
since pesticides assist the murderers, and those up to their wrists
in simple political blood, charged blood, the blood cast forth
were forced to drink
from the bees' bowl,
to share with bees

a fate,
the rim is busy, twitching, they talking
all about it.

It looked as if they were
a simple buzzing music box
and we could wind that spring
again
whenever it ran down

but found
a deeper wound of what
we only had one symptom of
and nothing
more of this was known.

9.

. . . how cool and lovely.

Time, the strangest thing that's going on,
the looping thing that happens in syntax,
subjunctively, conditionally, articulately
but never to return organically.

That fact means everything to us,
eventually being startling:
our own drowning.
Our dissolution.

The random! fallen into reality! just this way! look at it. A cabaret.
What have I done — it's yet again! More electronic dust? More
phoneme pulse? How much information do you need in the game of
information? How many proportionate subsets of interchange might

be suggested? Can the tiniest points be marked? I will reconstruct them, sized to the moment, while the evanescent loft of otherness surges with a cresting flash-flood, into this very narrow, inescapable spot.

10.

Why are the old elegies mainly
so busy, fussy-gussy like an over-fancy gown?
Figures coming and going, multiple
deities, songs, leaves, creatures'
account books, nymphs, other random,
mythological, allusive stuff,
often wordy, chock-a-block
with names, parades, and
ceremonies, with elongating lists,
syntaxes that spend time looping
around in all plausible directions
while nonetheless
traveling from this backwards
backwoods to forward?

Duh. Rhetorical questions.

11.

It was a perfectly clear night
over the lake.
Perfect sight for sky.
The grey-ish smudge
began, a little dirty
slowness. 21:30.

Soon, but not that soon,
because this was, as always,
boring in its stateliness,
the curved shadow, brownish,
seeped, tidal, arching
from the bottom of the moon.

At about one half, you,
seeing the red edge
(light-red, coral, yet
translucent) spread,
the coral-reddish color thickening,
could call it bloody.

The moon became heavy—
no dime-thin silver disk, this!—
it was green, solid, globular, clear.
Hanging, fully spherical, there.
Thus was, and is.
Will be.

Past midnight, logy,
dropping off suddenly,
I didn't see the waxing lunar shore.
It was enough to prove one
axiom of sidereal time.
I could not take many more.

FEBRUARY 2007–JULY 2010

Draft 104: The Book

There is no actual "the book," but it does exist.

The book withdraws into itself.

A book flakes, sometimes. Spins, spouts, charges, sputters.

Opening yod, its little eye, the book is awake.

The book, traveling backward, holds a smaller book, which it is reading.

A book is, however, an acceleration, or causes one.

"A" might turn into "The" book.

Only some books turn.

A door is a hinge. A book is another.

Opening a book is like tripping over a threshold.

A book is one gloss of the book.

Another book shines in the distance.

The book is the ledger of its whole account.

Every word adds up the word that never was.

Sometimes in a book, even with letters properly spaced, one finds a white rift open down the page.

And inside every letter is a tiny dark book.

Sometimes the book falls from your hands. You have entered into its dream; it
  seems to enter yours.

   It's about time you talked about the book. When you come
   to think of it.

One dark line down the page is not a book. But it could suggest you begin one.

   A book is the goal, but not just any book.

The season was fruitful. There was a book, ripening in the furrowed field.

   If you get thirsty harvesting, suck on a watermark.

The book, traveling backward, holds a smaller book, which it is reading. That
  book holds one smaller still.

   A is for aura, B is for book.

I loved he tried to put a lemon in the book! Because it wouldn't fit!

   A book in time saves nine. But rarely.

This sequence travels backward until the last thing visible is a dot. That dot is
  also a book.

   Inside the alphabet, a library.

A book can be indistinct.

   The book is, also.

Foreground syntax, entering the book. Decry syntax, escaping the book.

Write your book on the underside of another book.

A real book is a stone room.

You write your book; I'll write mine.

A book is surely the birth of an enigma.

Some book!

The book hinged open and closed, as if the letters, touching, read the words, the words the text.

So do not shut the open book.

If A is for aura, and B is for book, what is C?

For "three, three the rivals."

A book is a cut of several colors with warp threads hanging from it.

A book is a swirl of syntax written in light, spinning secularly.

It is a doll book and the book of the universe.

It whispers days, this book.

The house was quiet and the book was calm.

Which is the book? Which is the gloss?

The "the" of "The Book" is a tricky concept. But one doesn't just want "a."

There is a big eye in the middle of the book. It does not blink first.

[76]

This is it. This is The Book.

Yet really, don't be delusional.

Finally it is all related.

But it does not cohere.

A book notices. It looks out at you.

It's true that this book might finish; it's true it might go on.

What a book!

It snarls the translucence.

Full impasto ahead.

The page is slowly turning black.

The revulsion to a book, the attachment to the Book—totally explicable.

Each sibyl-syllable is made of darkening lightness. Ahhhhh, the darlings.

This is the from of the Book. Not its structure but its F R O M.

Its exodus.

JULY 2009, OCTOBER–DECEMBER 2009

[77]

Draft 105: Pilgrimage

No matter what, the awe of the mark

        Had dreamed of boxes   *a fear*
        to begin with? There was no   *setting it down, a risk. Of cul de sac, yet*
as soon as the hand touches the keys arrives *excess, the more, and then*
the awe and fear of   *not registering*
                              the matted infrastructure
        beginning; really, this is just a way   *of being awash*
flooded out. of speaking, words to say that there   *from nothing to everything*
from dessication to drowning,

        "was" something, for how (otherwise) *the force from inside seemed to*
    come from outside
        to enter this scattered yet saturated space

        without a point, no punctum, no
        boundary

 Of seeing a raptor snag a sparrow
right off the hedge on a narrow city street. All whorled
and feathered, evanescent
        just strangeness and porosity
        rapt. What hap

        was in and of these boxes, what space
        was to hopen (open? hope?) *these were dream queries*
                              like "nothing" ever before said
        in which enfolded matter   *colors on the clear air*
        not things, not concepts, nor textures *not black on white*
                      nor white on black
        but matter itself W A S
        unspeakable and indicative
bridge passage   *no key dominant*
        and solid. The urban

[78]

sparrow, the swooping Accipiter.
                    event, event, event constantly
aggressive.
        But it's true when I tell you that
        this sensation was not a namable thing.

Could this interlocutor be helper, say, or "angel"
        Which is why or what I had to name it *but can this word*
        over and over, again and again *ever be annulled?*

Behold! I said to it, that ghostly feathered
treacherous
luminosity   answering to *this spot of contact*
        the tertium quid, the in-between by

the boxes of
any day, plus dream of alternative setups
ones, twos   *obligating language to truth   to the outrageous*

NAMING

 where almost
every conclusion seems both right and wrong.

I N C I P I T is initial beginning
        Every piece of clutter compression,
        grit blown, random interactions *how odd is it that*

E X P L I C I T
        dilated vision. Must protect
        from that dispersion. Why?
 is the end

        Not sure, but need both shield

inexplicable   and veil, so the brightness of being

      and the insult of utter
      depression get buffered, bandaged or

      guarded from impact. Deprived
      of fullest penetration.

      Which could not be endured.
      Although it is desired.

      I pass the mound of scholar's rocks—
      odd formations with shunt holes

      through which eccentricities blow, inflating
      bulges of wisdom. And pass the setting sun—

the sound blue, blue dark, and solid black

No poem can finish. Which is the situation
of all poems in the set called poetry.
A resonance from the entire topology.

      Then the climb began
      and also began struggle.

      A person is climbing up the ladder
      made of an "angel"   *Mystical to think the alphabet*

BEING

just that ladder of letters

Give the stars
to the alphabet
the alphabet
to the stars.

It was real intensity, bleak *ascending*
rungs and indistinct receding end point

dissolving into a universe of atoms
The curls and whirls
The whorls and feathers
enraptured by the angelic raptor, whose goal is at once
darkening everything

inside the human
and the human bearing down   *and filling everything*
with light
both inside the inhumanity that
one affronts with rage and such implacable love as

be indistinguishable from indifference.
We hold and grapple. *Deep physics. Deep astronomy.*

A Metonic cycle takes 19 years.
And then the new moon and the full appear

on exactly the same day of the year
as they had done 19 years before.

Diasporas of letters
are pollen for honey

One is "lost" in this and unnerved *but the bees might have*
abandoned us. Don't abandon us! the outcry yet we abandoned them to pesticides

[81]

first   it builds slowly, *this is demonstrable by its debris*

  and suddenly the strugglers are "in deep"
in cataclysm, the black pages and the white pages mirror.
  unprepared and dazed by rapture.

The angel climbs upon substance, substance on angel   *ruthless*
  The one and the other
  hang upon each other
each yearning for the other's foreignness,

  climbing the fleshy and ineffable letter
as the pillar of fire burns the ladder
  climbing the fire burning the ladder.

January–February 2011

Draft 106: Words

—swervswerve!
but not as much as atoms.
The main thing we have in common is "restlessness."

Things do hold together, and
so does meaning
more or less.

glyphs   morse   pebbles   visionary   long   happenstance

sing-song   interlock   other   obdurate   something   memory

really   but also   diagnosis   ungainliness   what   never

barely   shards   thank you   haunted   between   and/or

trace   deeper   equally   where   of   midst

leaf   syntax   constitute   unpick   falsifies   bumpy

Signs under impingement
great lists+ of seasons' days   +grids
swirling, davening
far beyond vagaries
and Open 24 Hours.+   +intermittently.

The main word we have in common is "hap."

There is a clacking sound,
a weedy ditch, a pre-war map.
Words are blacked out,
or
they evoke inarticulate things

or
they stick in your gut, unsayable.

Something's coming loose. There is scattering
and the snap out of blurriness.
       There is brightness, too, and no
genre enough for it, even for its sudden shifting
         even for its affect.+   +impact.
And there are words
that become tremendous mantras,
doing fieldwork in ordinary language,
inventing what one found needed to be said,
and they reverberate+ for a long, long time.   +pontificate

Though words establish no exact center, with
      some words inside intangible centers,
         so words declare the variable as such,+   +permanent,
open what+ can never be scryed dependably.   +omens that

      This also gives rise to resonance. +   +reciprocity.

Low ostinato enfolded in itself gets
excited+ by+ its own vibratos of implication.   +extruded + from
Structurally "errata." Generically "mixed."
      Enjoyably the "noise" of "clumps."
        Seriously "negation."

Plus whole lives of "ands" inside the work+   +the unintelligible
    await openings
within the out-flung surge of cosmic time.

Another word we have in common is "sideral."

So that

the whole universe and every sociable part of it
pulses semi-translatable messages
maybe in words,
maybe words being part of that, one imagines
tintinnabulations
but hears only
the rumble of materials
where+   +given
everything equals Being+   +Begin
even what seems to not.

The unknown
in exfoliation.+   +federation.

It is changing as it speaks.+   +we speak.
It is not totally our language
but it is+ speaking word to word   +we are
correlating overlaps of syntaxes.

Words matter; things are discussable.
We cannot not think so.
        Alternative is unthinkable.
        Or worse still—thinkable it is. Suppose words
do not matter.
Then would we stop making them?
And as best we can?
No.
The motivation?
A wager so precise it makes Pascal's look petty.

Let it all in, fissure, fracture, and broken shard, let the mobile
        in. Leap into this excess ripe and snide, the compost thick
                with overlays of conjunction, and leap
                (is it the same leap?

consider the question later)
into one or another void.

How? I'm glad you asked.

Like fairy tales, the poem demands the collection of tasks.

Unlike them, you cannot count on three's.

Gather and respect the endless ordinal rips.

And appreciate the keening micro-tones

in empathy with dark news read in the darkness.

All of the above gives rise to vertigo,
and the poem is energized+   +enlarged
by that.

Might even postulate other intelligences+   +inferences
(half-baked, like us) capable
of belated reconstructions,+   +reconsiderations,
might postulate occurrences parallel to this
from modes+ of similarly intent   +moans
witness.

Not epigrams with a twist
of rhyme, nor lyric's
soaring+ soundings. Finally   +solemn

portage   creased   thus   what   there fragments

did   evident   long   at least   I   but

multiple   O   stubborn   besides   existed   can't

as if   &   out   joists   whatever   Sign

rubble   project   how?   telling   exigent   tangle

boundaries   shatters   it   ███████   anything   turned.

And at 4:32 exactly
              the wind that's blowing fiercely
          hits such down swoops as a short-eared owl
is like a night train with that longtime faraway hoo—.
Nothing is stranger than life. Except, maybe, languages.
With words, the world
is more than is the case.
How could it not
be just that way.

AUGUST–OCTOBER 2011

Draft 107: Meant to say

If one talks of depth, it's not necessarily psychologizing things.
The inside of the object might be social . . . .

P. INMAN

Meant only to list, one and one and one, wonder. But found I needed verbs.
And then I needed time.

Meant to note the heavy doors
whose weight, without having been there, one can only pretend to intuit.

Meant to erase half the words or more
but couldn't bring myself to do it.

Wanted to know about making art and telling the truth.
Why this engineered apple tastes dull, how did we get here
and did we decide to?
or else what flood of slough
drowned us where we stood.

Meant to make the stitches more overt, patches and their overlap.
But aesthetically.

Meant to sketch every day, and thus note more, much more,
so far away from what is called "the center," it might as well be here.

Question: "Looking back, what did you learn?"
Answer: "What a small amount of metal it takes to kill you."
Meant to say: "Cost that out."
It isn't as if this thought has gotten nowhere?

Conjunctures of intensity
play out as dispersion. So meant to make a poetics.
The way people do.
But it never included everything I wanted.

Meant to take webbed strings
and watch small articulations,
meant more mystery, and more humility.
What I meant might have been more saturated in
the understanding of paralysis.

Meant to write biographies of obscure objects and their provenance.
What is beyond the sublime?
What beyond the old poems with their alarming
Preponderance of white marble
And green travertine?

Meant to have spelled *Dinggedicht* correctly,
but didn't.

The lapis, the amethyst, the turquoise,
the soft brown velvet sack,
symbols of other gifts, all unspoken
all under-acknowledged, never
enough questions asked,
Depression glass,
the carrion crows settling, satisfied, on road kill,
The white chip off a deep blue bowl from France,
Tin tea trunk. Little toy it was.
That kind of thing—you know what I mean.
A list of unaccountable items, totally yours.

Some are lost. Others list. A wake of themselves,
they send as much forward
as they can.
But I saw that file only in shreds.
Meant to get more from it.

Meant to mention the poem is always in motion.
Always moving away, is what I meant to say.

What I meant was some painful, almost implausible point
between being abandoned and —what?— assumed into our human-ness.
This whole era has lived in denial,
affirming or sanctioning genocide and destruction.
Meant to say, what now.
Who is the intermediary for what? I meant to notice.

I meant to create the kind of beauty that was not beautiful
in the way I did not want. This left me without
much of what I was once meant to do,
so had to change my mind.

Meant to keep better records.
Meant to ask more questions.

Coming from time, webbed further in time,
to get singed, torn, used up, wrangling.
That's what I meant.
What does the characteristic feeling
of debris and twisted twisting actually say?

Meant, I meant to start and
to startle myself. It was so.

Trample the vanity of the poem!
Do you need this piece of string?
I saved it for you, for the knot and length to work on,
under, over, twist, and let it hold
so you could weave it in the webbing that
you keep too; it is your archive as well as mine, this little
piece of nothing, this

part of the imaginary whole.

Would it have helped to be less careful, or more?
I would have liked
to understand the choice better. Meant to.

Should there be fewer moments of the heightening of art?
I meant a greater ambivalence.
Meant to keep on saying, What do you do this for?

And meant to stay in the ungainly spot where too-little and too-much
struggle between an open fright.

Meant to finish. Now it is not clear what I meant
or what I mean by that.
But readiness is right.

I meant to let the poem pass into its particular autism,
a compound paralysis of overloaded desires.

Can one overcome one's own cowardice?
Meant to ask this.
Plastic no longer means malleable.
It means a voluminous tax on the ocean.

Trample the vanity of the poem. It is a smudge on the page.
If nothing more, could walk between the lines.
The words I found
made other words
their interlocutors.

Here's the twisted key.
What kind of an event is this?
Shouldn't all writing be utopian

but also plausible?
The failures are ethical they are rhetorical they are political, what
aren't they?

Yet how could I limit the call I'd made?

Ring the bell.

Ring the bell again.

This thing is the "only poem" you'll ever need
but you'll need it (no matter who writes it), over and over.

July–August 2010

Draft 108: Ballad and Gloss

The rising moon loomed up, abrupt.
It filled the arc of sky.
Orange, grand, then laser white,
It bleached the stars nearby.

A thick book opened
for these moonshine mixtures
and bright-dark pages pulsed
with moon-phase pictures.

The wary rover began to track
those wayward stories once again
through clover clouds of coded twists
that split and list and never end.

> The terms are set, but never fully so. There is the world and the watcher
> or wanderer, and there is the sense of pressure or presence that must be registered,
> as if this figure encapsulated the wonder and anger of many others, who are not
> there. This might constitute a critique of the gestures to be made. And at every
> moment, there will be oddities of the journey.

Cribbed in a tod of winter ivy,
lies a frozen mouse
curled in the tiny garden
at the front of the house.

Up the next block—23rd Street
directly above Locust—
is a patchy smudge of concrete
mortared differently from the rest.

The cement indents,
the sidewalk cracks.
One cosmos resting on one shim.
Are there meanings to these facts?

One cosmos, a simple word choice, for there may be many. What anything rests on,
we cannot postulate. Insofar as one plans for solidity, it seems appropriate to
mention that we are mainly space (between atoms) as well as water (98%). There are
unimaginable distances to cover, even to swim, just to get to the next unit. This is
inside the inside: "we" interrupt, if briefly, the porous jumpiness of particles. Dark
energy 74%, dark matter 22%, and for the rest . . . ?

The shim is pi, the decimal
unrepeating: 3.141592653589793.
Etc. Numbers go forward, letters loop back—
related practices of infinity.

Mathematics as such is not the point, although pi has gone, through
computer computations, to a giggle or gaggle or googol of numbers
(Google it), and there is no pattern. Could that mean endless? These shims, the
irregular bits, the uneven, the odd, and the wobble render any self-important
claims of regularity ridiculous. Pi is just a little shim, a useable proposition,
fitting our formula for it, and, as squeezed this way or that, almost perfect, yet
absolutely inexact. Luckily it's like a healthy child, active and sturdy. As it
approaches itself, it creates a polyhedron almost into its limit circle.

Onto the yellow pine planking
dropped a spot of cerulean blue
where Goodman did his painting.
It's still there, after him, in situ.

This blue spot is just one
among multitudinous dots, each
outlining any polygon
that searchers might reach.

This blue pointillist moment
refracts and prisms
whole spectra of colors—
and we are lost inside them.

Here are unmet agendas
and folds that fail of neatness.
There are many loose ends
and episodes of incompleteness.

Puzzles of art half solved.
Rhymes barely rescued from the mess.
This array is really unresolved:
oranges, blue, the moon, a spot, my no-y yes.

> "No" is the resistance before this began. The "yes" occurred intermittently.
> "Image" might be a half-rhyme for" orange." "Orage" too, but in another
> language. Or "ange." Considering what we really believe in, that could be a
> willful choice, not accurate in the normal way, as something actually seen, but
> acknowledging a feeling beyond normalcy. Is it too convenient, too conventional to
> deploy this ineffable "Angel"? Not sure what to say to that. The imagination of the
> concept answers to something that we know. Is the word acceptable? Any word is an
> angel, really. Let that be some sort of an answer.

Let's just get one rhyme for "orange"!
You know the way certain women
take on any foolish challenge?
—It arguably rhymes with "lemon."

Agreeably. Agrumily. Lemon—
to symbolize the clearest real:
yellow ovoid, pocky skin,
a plate, a glistening peel.

But by this standard, poets must
choose only the Rectitude Font.
Yet other words peek out from
the dictionary. That's their wont.

> *Peek or peep. A sound or a look. Undertone or overtone. The word behind the word*
> *Lemon, leman, limen, lumen. There are lights so strong that when they fall over the*
> *book, the page is shadowed in the glare. There are after-images and floaters. What*
> *does it mean to say that something's clear? It means not seeing everything that's*
> *there.*

Something's always doubling the double.
Shadows of trace remain intent.
Something explores its own excess.
Something pulses, never spent.

Littler and littler,
seely after seely
only a fine-meshed, mesh-fine net
can deal with this kind of real. Really.

Poetic technology always registers
smallness in the count.
With large-bore machinery, tiny details
are filtered through and out.

I cannot solve what is done in my name. They send 100 million to the killers
from my insistent taxes; I send $500 to some other side. This has been going on for
years now. Cannot solve, cannot absolve . . . And "orange" is not an absolute; it has
been worked with—for it itself is generally hybrid. It comes from bud unions and tree
grafts and sometimes spontaneous mutations. Fusions of root-stock with something
from elsewhere. Much more rarely from seeds. What then counts as "normal"?

Many a doctor thought the spleen
was simply second-rate,
To operate and take it out
would hardly dent a body's fate.

Imagine their surprise to learn
"that this was not the case" at all.
Embarrassed Experts say they're stunned
to find that little organ's gall.

See also histones. Scientists had thought that histones were just a storage spool, "a
passive framework for the DNA" –a holding system for matter of far greater
import. And yet, surprise again, "this is not the case." One starts to wonder
what ideological assumptions they routinely begin with.

Then one day a Red Admiral,
Vanessa Atalanta,
landed on my head and held there
working its antennae.

At night the butterfly became a ray
that flapped its meaty intensity
flying low over my head
and followed, oceanic, chasing me.

Day and night, consciousness and dream, the outside and the inside. No way can you
separate the two; the news is interlaced. The adequacy of language produced
has, somehow, to be worthy of it.

Night and Day outlined each other's topic
and were tangled, and even amusing,
Shoelaces! imagine that as optic.
Regard their beauty.

Imagine any other "me" long gone,
the clumps of us, the surds,
the lumps, fool fatedness of all
spires, cycles, works and words.

Now one watches downfalls and implosions, written on and bound, held to our
body, as if ritual objects, with leather straps. These boxes of lead are pressed
upon us, bound to our very glands. We must bear them, carry them, though they are
heavy and encumbering. Poisonous. There is nothing to do besides trying to unpick
our complicity, that tight-bound, tight-wrapped knot. Painful to write such allegory,
whose other name is reality.

The traveler becomes the road itself
wand'ring round and through.
The bramble tracks from star to star
produce her as hypotenuse.

There's Orion, crisp, the hero.
How can that be comfortable?
Although it may seem to most
as something perfectly normal.

racing streaks, points, gleams, elations
the oddness both above us and within,
we are marked thus, saturated
one odd smudge to another. Skin.

> It is a condition of gathering into the array of relations that goes by the name of
> "otherness," some done deal, anyway, other wise, otherhow, that light webs
> touching my arm hairs as I move through the early morning are a reminder of
> intricacies that cross our paths, of skills, aptitudes and worlds in which are many
> things that we might understand if only not irrevocably to harm.

Hence the story turns its spindle,
twists with endless fibrous spate.
Nothing is settled, nothing yet finished.
All is latent, potentially template.

To begin here. Begin again.
Now? At the end? That's just absurd.
No. It's so the story will play out
again, or maybe differently, in every word.

JULY–AUGUST 2011

Draft 109: Wall Newspaper

I. Of the Dead

March was the month when fissures opened.

It was a completely clean hallucination. It all made a kind of sense.

Larger rifts were earth wide. Smaller were local hairline cracks. There were multiple scales of events, unsorted, uneven.

Who can evaluate the destabilizing, limp paralysis, the thin shim under the everyday, and then the worse normalization?

She said "the canary in the mine field." The phrase was totally logical.

"Mann geboren frei ist" had been graffito'd on the train station. The "chains" clause was left uncited.

Water poured into the streets, dragging everyone under. Drought became endemic desertification, humus to dust.

Poetic autonomy never existed. In a few weeks, a dead zone had to be declared.

Any yeast that's left will take decades to work.

The instruments are ghosts of themselves.

Here include the base and superstructure of me. But of course can't draw a line, one on one side.

What is being breathed, when breathing in this air?

The interconnections among things remained unspoken, untraceable, inextinguishable, like the smell of mold.

Chains are cumbersome, enslaving; links are necessary, and some are irrevocable.

When it gets revealed as jerry-built decisions, poor oversight, technological hubris, malfeasance and profiteering, then deflect attention.

To what, depends on site-specific calibrations: to claims of your "excessive" anger, to formally choreographed "apologies," to crimes of mimesis, to saleable scandals and titillations. Occasional scapegoating. Scatters of random amulets. Perhaps analysis. The odd exemplary sentence. Exchanges of experts.

Slowly I leave a much-loved place I probably won't return to.

[100]

What is the target genre? "Stony rubbish"? This is a textbook case. Hold on tight.

The question of bees. The question of bats.

"Nature suddenly appeared like an emptied room." Pencil marks up the wainscoting, some child's sizes, dates. The room, however, was splintered, the child crushed.

"Do you please remember me?" the long-ago asked from her shadow. This is a collective though partial account, after the detonation of frameworks.

So carefully biting around the meaty pericarp of Apple, she stood there.

That woman is called irksome.

It might even snow, end March, early April.

When Three Mile Island went, everyone stood outside and became an instant expert on the prevailing winds.

The surge in the discursive system was so enormous that one could not walk, drink, eat, even breathe without feeling endangered by its uncontrolled electricity.

What's in it? What's in it for them? But these questions eroded, frayed, abraded.

Then the actual system surfaced, with its un-degradable plastic, with "odds and ends in constant flux manipulated by desire and fear."

Some have deliberately made the seeds infertile. This is a consequence of profit taking.

The future will wonder "what the fuck were they thinking."

Three languages, but now she could not speak, a symptom of her dying.

Olfactory hallucination as I wake: the smell of coffee brewing.

Being "born," as Olson said, "not of the buried but these unburied dead." "You must change your life." Me alone, or who?

Poetry—something "replete with signifiers and gibberish." Makes a kind of sense.

They are predicting a lot of snow up the East Coast.

But I don't feel bad. Can't apologize (too much) for this pock-marked landscape. Nevertheless, I feel terrible. "Why? April is the coolest month!" Can you say "parallel universe"?

Occasional flowering is a normal characteristic. The poem's not about the baby Christ child just because the word frankincense is in it.

Severe choices of brilliant play. Temporality happens every day.

Let's tie the hands of the assholes.

Alternative life: orthopedic surgeon. Hobby: trekking.

Keep your valuable properties with you at all times.

The social world drained back into the work; the dam was over-passed.

CHAOS BECAME A WAY OF LIFE.

Canvas bags with a special logo got distributed to the task force.

Meantime, I have other plans. So to speak.

Does anyone here really know why he saw poets as "horses"?

Q. teased that he would write his memoirs and call it My Lie.

The exhibit featured a colonial baroque silver teapot in the shape of a giant turkey. That level of extraction was almost startling.

A "secular Jewish Pegasus" would be what?

The sheer excess of the untransparent impossible has no verb right now. Sorry.

A long time ago, when things got bad, they'd grind up the inner layer of tree bark—pine only, a soft wood—and bake it with rye flour. How long ago a time was that?

Here include the dominant, residual and emergent of me.

Here, rhizomic nekuia.

"Let the dead bury their dead" being completely impossible—now what?

Being half-dead—a strained, self-estranged under-acknowledged fear? Particular "end of world" apocalyptic prophecies get media play.

On the other hand, the radioactive waste and debris will arrive on these shores in about one year. With the bare hands—plus a few pair of latex gloves to go around. Sea to shining sea.
Our lives are privatized, all except our private lives. This has been reviewed and is legal.
Are there real differences between here and there?
The sand was pocked and garbaged with tar clumps. Will we rupture and pull to shreds the ribbon of life simply by default?
Even those one wished to idealize were full-scale despoilers.
It would starve you more slowly.

We live here in this time, saturated with a few other times, and some few people. We're friends or whatever. The between is where we are.
This is a confused sadness, where you can't even feel that sadness.
The page, the door, the wall; whatever can be learned, it's pinholes, although "the word," she said, "leads inward into itself." This is only half the story, although perhaps the more attractive half.
We're propelled into linked emergencies with unintended fallout.

My skin imagines lines—
there's me and him, and
me and it, her, us, you, and the time
we have been together when we've
foraged in what is, and
some things got smashed, and
some are rejoined, and
we quote from each other,
sister and brother.
Do not turn away.

Reader, if any! We are a symptom.
We are mirrors of our own corpses.
This is closest to darkness.
Surrender to it.

[103]

The stone, as in all Moravian cemeteries, was exactly equal to the others, set flush with the ground. But I found it by the shells encircling her name. Chatter to fill up time on the death watch—but what to say? Student: "Why would God make His people suffer such great deals?" In this colorful escapade, A is for Apple, B is for black hole. One to ten billion in one fell swoop. These socio-lexical sparklers, these sounds and codes pulse in saturated rhythmic segments. Makes a lot of sense. Let's rank the rambles. And together we woke, readjusted warmly, and fell back asleep. It didn't seem a stroke of luck at the time—just, like, normal. Surf-intense danger; buried clots on the mud flats. Alternative life: social geographer. Hobby: fencing. "Are you keeping up with yourself, or not?"

Jade is extremely refractory by its nature. K. missed his mother, why he wore ambiguous clothing and his hair long like a girl's. People kept saying "she" about him. And there was a time when L. had cropped hair, chose boys' clothing, and got harassed in ladies rooms whenever she went to pee. Call the question. I want to bleed this over the margins of every single page.

Ribbons—Green White Violet—Give Women Votes. Makes a kind of sense. I feel I've barely lived my real life. Once the word "feminist" surfaced, all hell broke loose in the comment stream. The eye zoomed up from underneath as if a lens were buried underground. Men in work clothes and in suits threw women. Picked them up, threw them, throwing hard with the intent to break them. Terrible sleep, my heart then racing. Mushy day, with a dank chill under the surface. Ze (xe?)—another entrant into the pronoun problem. Hir as a solution for the possessive? May I pronoun myself—e.g., I, Tiresias, the King Self? We own or own up to what parts of social gender? Paid on a sliding scale. Then I thought that a number 12 might be coming, so ran that last half block and finally made it home. And one day in

Bethlehem, I washed H.D.'s grave, cleaning off the lichen with my wet bandana.

Chicken at 40,000 feet, 4 Perrier, 3 Tampex, 2 cabernet, and one movie where it's a blonde and a bimbo decoding [irony].™ He had a student who thought "The Oven Bird" was about Thanksgiving. Makes a kind of sense. "A little doll is the solution." To what? So women hold up half the sky—who cares? Fragmentation implies a theory of wholes. But possibly not. The pencil was invented the year after Shakespeare was born. Wherever did you read that? The secret to cooking turkey is to turn it off quite early, letting it sit for a long while in the warm oven. It's beginning to feel like a serious snow. Those were imitation or decorative oghams, whose marks, according to experts, actually said nothing.

This work, she said, is a darting arrow. There is such fervent, obsessive interest in policing women and in punishing women. Why did these years happen the way they did? What are the relationships among different margins? The lawyer's pen was printed "Helping people preserve their wealth" in small gold letters. "One best-selling book!" (what're you a writer for if you don't want one?) "you'd make a lot of money—then you could do poetry, or whatever you want." Alternatively, low production values. The glue showing. No set level. And the rips. De-story the book; destroy the page but in the gaps, two-homedness, Zweiheimigkeit. Mapped "in these labyrinths of terrible differences—the dilemmas of truths."

Mis-en-abyme-ishly,
she seizes the pages of discarded books
she weeding she shewing she feeling she seeing
pages of the scarred books in which
"the unspeakable words never cease their subversive action."
Though never quickly.
If not now, when?

"I hold my honey and I store my bread . . ."
There was an attic
& then a second door into a second attic.
The airports of the living face the airports of the dead.
To run before walking—that's what she wanted.

The ordained woman remarked categorically: "St. Paul didn't write that!" But as it's canonical, now what? The generic matchbook on the sidewalk was printed "THANKS." Despite the delicacy of edelkayt, you must articulate your rascal side. T. is writing on one of those lost women artists. She told me who, but I forget her name. A man and a woman get into a taxi. I lost my nice cosmetic bag in that very taxi. Everything is a thread.

Ends up at 28.5 inches. This year's Philly record, and the third overall. 4181 is the 19th Fibonacci number. It's the whole nine yards. I'd suggest the word "human" or the word "person." She wrote a section of her piano trio for toys. They changed the instruments mid-performance, and played toy violin, cello, and piano reflectively, like bits of girlhood thinly pinging. 2000 blackbirds baked in the sky. Is going beyond gender through gender enough? I make action plans. I plan my own loss.

Ze is the sibyl in her fetid bottle. The answer to the question is delusional: "I want to live again!" I learned today it's older hens that lay those larger eggs. How about equality of questioning. Equality of straining. Of struggling. But then—it is not yet equal. So act as if? Then what?

The sounds a-blur confuse the statement. Hearing aids don't clarify when many voices speak at once. The scherzo is scored as if the whole orchestra were tuning, scratching, randomly plucking. That's a tough egg to follow! Another genre: epyllion. Not this one. Or is it? Full moon sex. Makes a lot of sense. Choose the phrase "female-bodied people." After her lecture on women's post-dictatorship civic status, a man stood up to ask "What about the penis?"

That "best seller" woman didn't credit that consciousness might follow from such operational choices. She was far too rich to think that! So much has happened. Quite suddenly. A snake struck Lady-dog, and I cried "HELP" in the dream. Thus I woke, stunned by the sound of that desperate interior voice. Anyway, it's time now. It's really time.

III. FIRE SURF

Thereupon gigantic figures, earth and clay, announced that I stood with my feet only half planted. But the surface of the earth was in motion. I thought I had constructed these images, but detritus and its muddy tide had, in fact, made me. With its oil-gritty crescent strips and nipple-puckered seed buttons, the eucalyptus is a mightily combustible tree. I saw rogue energy; I saw piles of smashed debris; I saw the ribbon-braided holding place for river, but in this season being weedy furrowed dust in a wide, flat gully.
I was wood and could be burned.
"We have our marching orders. We will be playing the killed civilians."
For a while, half sleep, it seemed much better, but given insomniac anxiety, it was not in fact better.
Bright lights refracted back downward under the blue-black clouds into one of the world's tiniest airports. The wheels made their dark ripping sound as the bottom opened. Still, I'm endlessly making up for lost time.
Shunt the folded twists up and down the synapse; there were questions, but it was simpler just pointing to that spot.
Plans—big. Follow-thru—compromised.
No blades, awls, large shampoos, or gels. Headquarters miscalculated. We must stick with it. So much has already been invested.

[107]

He responds to the downturn by more intense tactics of marketing.
Photoshop satiety.
Brightness, seductive pouting, chiaroscuro—how to trigger some-one's desire.
Mortgage companies began to destabilize, then to fail. Real assets did not match their liabilities.
The ogham slice and one more notch on the tree-thick stone—
is this a real one, or a fake?
Who knows how to read this language?
All the big firms, Morgan Stanley, Lehman, Bear Stearns, held artful arrangements of debts and slice-and-dice notes so intricately segmented that it was all finally untrackable.
The attack of the difficult spread sheet.
Whatever was guaranteeing solvency might have been the same thing over and over.
(Buzzer sound.)
(Ignore buzzer sound.)
All of them making big money, big plunder,
smash and grab, a pretty ugly ferment that foretold the rest,
and impossible to ignore (one would have thought).
What one would have thought got squandered.
There was no lack of telling, and
the operable lexicon
couldn't turn away
but it couldn't intervene either.
The houses were broken, the walls fell open.
This is, of course, a pyramid scheme, so the system began to collapse.

They were just rogue soldiers. They were just bad apples. There were unfortunate mis-calculations. An official apology will be sent.
On this stela, the motif of the handshake with the dead.
Jade cannot be carved with metal tools.
S. is worn down with chemo.

And now she cannot speak. Only by hard mineral abrasive, worked into a paste.
That company's name was Chimera Capital.
I saw the sign. I was there.
The stylized masculinity of the noir does make a certain sense.
Mannered so beautifully under its scrim of attractive doubt, packing heat, it's almost comedy.
In life, however, the firewall is discontinuous. It has already become rubble.

Therefore it is good
to have companions

even if those were few
and sometimes unavailable.
If only time had not passed

the way it did, dribbled in bits,
us slogging through, oddly
glad it's over—but think of that.

It is good also
to feel compassion
inside the dream and out of it.

He just keeled over. It was beyond understanding.
There was an exchange of birds between the living and the dead.
"As they exit, they strike an antique cymbal, which reverberates in unison
with the cello harmonic."
All those incipits were historiated letters.
This poem has been given a lot of ink.
Prosody: modulations of the void.
I lost one lapis earring.

Singular sadness, far in excess of the object.
What the genre said.

The news was such that I learned the word for slaughter, massacre:
la strage.
Fire use in hominids — a benchmark.
Sign at the diner take-out — "ham bagel."
"Effortlessly" they said, "she effortlessly transmutes the personal into
the political." Oh, please.
This will be a surgical strike. We have very accurate data where they
are.
He etches the places you are not supposed to notice — storage units,
airport scanners, rooms with no windows, shipping containers,
concrete barriers.
In their place — all smoke, some luck, but barely, the only thing
saving them, three-alarm fire, was a double brick wall.
Waking at 5, I saw a pink moon setting. Pouring over the numbers
and letters of meaning, one forces the tiniest marks and nets to hold
this splay. Inflame, inflamed, inflaming images.

The green hose snakes through the pocky grass, but with a crimp in
it. Uncrimp it and get the backlogged water to pour out.
Turn one's pockets inside out, push open the corners to find the dust,
the grift, the grit and fuzz of lint we are.
It is frightening, this part of the world's work — of a technical useless-
ness (so far as accounting goes). But the articulation of multiple
complexities, the saturations of syntax within lexicons, the synapses'
unpredictable pulsation
become portal to a hard and puzzling insistence.

    "The voices of the children,
        singing in the dome above."
Alongside
    "anxious about the market of everything

About the sound of our voices in the cavernous dome"

Odic abyss and Odos—the pilgrimage. Take the whole as a spirit journey into the real.
My friends and I have come to stay / to visit in another life. This is a powerful place I am looking to live. Magnetic. Who is it that turns up! You!

This is a different kind of counting. Bring me my arrows of desire.

IV. BY WATER

Food is manipulated, water is manipulated, education is manipulated, ownership, land, resources, medicine, heavily manipulated. Prisons are a profitable service industry. This is a double-entry ledger. But you'll have to gather, prune, and repack this array—the boat is leaving in twenty minutes! Grab what you need—do you know what that is? Throw it in the suitcase, stuff it into the plastic trash bag. We have to get on that boat. No, but maybe we don't. Maybe we should stay. What ever shall we do? Hard to watch the dithering. The scrum at the dock. What do we need? It really is a pity. Call it the "whatever." Whatever bits there were, folded and crumpled together. Consider this a cultural heritage. Dead yellow-bellied sapsucker on Pine. I used to be a "Sagittarius" and now am that other one, the new sign. It was (as they say now) a "mute point." Just leave the water on the moon alone!

V. THUNDERSTORM DAWN

I woke to a thunderstorm dawn, a yellow-gray dim with thin rising and polka dots of pinkish petals driven off the bloomed, blown cherry.
It rained for twenty hours. No more drought for us. At least right now. Dream of much confusion with suitcases. Could wake to find the

same. What a story board! There's no particular "elsewhere."
But this new social subject, neither individual nor collective—isn't quite me, either. More pronouns needed? Just saying.
This cup was made by one of the Little Masters.
At South Square Market, when they mist the veggies, a small loud-speaker plays "Singin' in the Rain."
All your hard work will soon be paid off.
"It's plain American that *talented* cats and dogs could read."

Making a list—but always missing an item. There was always something else. I couldn't identify what, but one felt it there. Blurred. Uncanny.
Bony travelers
scrabble across the looped and wayward scroll,
decoding or suffering
overgrown paths and scrub oaks,
and hinging, half-hung, half-off broken doors.
They swing, riding a riffled book.

Who was the third one, and the fourth?
I needed to bring them into focus.
Was that a man or was that a woman?
Interesting to think.

Alternative life: cellist. Hobby: my vegetable plot.
It seems perfectly clear that we will not outlast the on-earth years of the dinosaurs. Though this was a longish time—is that consolation? or not? Unthinkable?
The works and days, the sediments and glistening minerals, the fuzz and furze—it will make a thick and blasted palimpsest, yet perhaps only marginally readable. Who will decode it?
Every one of us so stuffed already, yet still trying to fill the void: religion, food, fat, glut, candy, shopping, stuff. Nothing is what I want. Well, just this.

Au lecteur de l'avenir! Salve! Here it is! I am decorating nothing. I am stating.

The dry stream down the rock side suddenly flowed to flood. An incredible storm. Afterwards, picked up the unripe tomatoes blown to the ground.

The storm discharged that pent-up electricity. We could all finally sleep. Not the same rain as yesterday, but a new dripping drupe shape, in droopy drops.

Cf. that second and third beside you, that third and fourth, wandering in cadence. A familiar cadence of familiar droning. Intensities of keening create humming.

Deiknumena: here are the many mysteries; these are the things shown.

Here they are!

When the ants ate the dead bat, they ate it all the way down, including the bones. There was no bat skeleton left. There was nothing but sated ants. Which is something after all.

The page, just printed, feels warm to the touch.

To make fried green tomatoes with the falls, use corn meal or polenta for the coating.

There were five military over-flights per day—fighter jets cracking over the top of the hill. That was right before the newest, freshest war.

"There was a brief break before the beating resumed,
and my first impulse was to cover my ears, but then I thought,
'If this man is crying, shouldn't someone hear him?'"

The mystical
        lettristic elaborations
of numbers couldn't.
        A net made only of documents

couldn't. Nor, curiously,
could the mourners. The tasks:
    to listen, to identify & to respond.
Marvel to walk in language within being.
    Even cloaked by desperation and by rage.
I can no longer resist
what this is
and what it has become

in all elaboration
and beyond-itself complexity.
Let it begin again,
begin against again.

An early poem was called "The War Years." And it is still.
My right eye's blurry, filled with something thin, irritating, and
    folded.
It is a translation without an original.
"They baffle me, too. That's all I'm painting for."

Now's the time when people post their news upon a wall.
Choose talismans to hang above their desks.
Citations. Aphorisms. Gifts of the ever-receding angel.
Museum postcard of a glistening lemon. "Voyage autour de mes
    cartes postales."
They look. We look. At it. The full array.
Of metamorphosis, tolerance, curiosity, attentiveness; of humility,
    conjunctures and juxtapositions. Of clashes and debates. Of
    pain.
Write messages, press send.
The journey did not end. I arrived almost nowhere and knew
    almost nothing. But still it did not end. So that—

"I would like to be able to write a book that is only an Incipit,
    that maintains for its whole duration the potentiality of the
    beginning, the expectation still not focused on an object."

Aura. Aurora. Prototype, all being preamble to the first figure,
like a documentary, only different.
Selva oscura meet obscure self,
wandering among itchy plants and between brambles,
a confrontation
with the fact of a question.
To follow there, "discovering new ways of folding."
But never, luckily, enough.

So that my nudity
and the rumbles of language
in my curly gut morph into
magnetism and polyphonic eros.
And thus or thereupon
one recent summer day,
I found a long pubic hair
growing twisted and wiry
right from my listing ear.

Hum hum humn, hymn and bong,
detritus and vertigo in sentences and lines,
you ethical ecology of vectors: you've stunned
me yet again with that incandescent
mix of arousal, illogic and grief I call my time.
And coming to this endless wall of volatility
that thing becomes a name.

Begin with any letter. Swallow and disgorge.
"this rrrr   to be a river"
"rien   n'aura eu lieu   que le lieu"

"She carries a book
of the unwritten volume"
that fills and empties pulse and surge.

Singing the exergue
nmnmnm—going backwards
half-hazardly mn und nm & utterals from
the knotted self, suffused with such a
dirty, yearning light, with such
ungainly LIFHT, with such
clustering reverberation,
it underscored the toll.

"Wer, wenn ich schriee, hörte mich denn. . . . "
"We have constructed ruins
to be reborn out of."

APRIL–JULY 2011

Draft CX: Primer, a selection

Letters, a preface.

   to the matted mast of alphabet

This is a work from bursts of the visual in the verbal, and round about again, verse visa. This is a work primed with letters, with colors, read and seen, red and scene, the magic and oddity of daily life ripped to bits

          rotting and steaming, filled with red-tipped worms. Just the daily, as in dated blocks. fluttering letter-farfalle un-cocooned. To see the letters sweetly, but with surge behind them. This is creation, combustible, sensuous, pleasures giving pleasure. Rebar of the infrastructure. The Alpha and Omega. A wry powerful wraith. Pairing letters, paring words, peering over the A   byss, the B byss of feather hemp pot (poet) determinatives. As in m no am em, O, on the SE corner to BE. HHow does one learn to see the difference, in a new alphabet—the minrness of the detail. A dot, a yod-like qshift or change and difference, alteration, shift, palette sounded here and there. (h) (h) (h) (h) plus   X, its pluck and jube.

Crackle sounds and sonorities. Each letter (R. C. M.) an epistle TO the one who looks at them. *as if the letters, touching, read the word, the word the text.* Gripping each other. N as in begin. A is followed by Y. Some letters fold over themselves, facing each others' halves: H. T. W. Perhaps O. The letters rise as if propelled on smoke, the leaves burn, the flecks of autumn go to ash; this book dissolves into its making. Q.V. to all of it.

   There is packing. There is oddity. There is conjunction. There's even Qwerty. Pessoa's was Azerty.
   And there we are again—the alphabet. For the n-th time
   The books compost. The letters detach. A again, again they say, for apple. The appeal and appel. Apt. The W of Cassiopeia now an M. And

Zone. This is very odd. UneXpected. Which is just to say: This Book is one of them, it is.

Some of it is funny. The fframed, the is-lated, the sudden brought together with others of the same. Of that ilk. Ilk of ilkiness. Honestly—the letters NSEW. Cardinals. Who knew? O and I are, they say, the most (poetic)™. This letter is life, iota-iota. A dot is as extensive as π wherein all the numbers, unrepeating, are gathered to a point. En plus, E, Etc. These are letters and they are tinged with what they are. R.

The N's and Y's and Xing place and R's dominate
but sometimes R is dropped from the work
I mean from the word
with odd
e-sults.

As they tumble up their alphabetic stair, as the petal hits the mettle, I go down the passage into a mirroring zone. It is as if these made themselves. They wanted to be. Faced with the bright alphabet, the letters want to say themselves, their bits. Open the packages! Turn it all inside out! A process of scraping, of ripping, of pasting. Wanting the insides of things, their undersides. The package inside out. The layers of pressing. The cardboard. Mite and mote. It's being like that.

They glean, they unpack and layer, they are a little thick, they deturn images, they frame and reframe the debris. They gleam.

And they reach and touch, and I am in their house.
We meet, collapse and tumble.
One raucous interface,
porous, yod to yod, one and one,
and each to each.

DECEMBER 2009 & AUGUST 2010

Draft 111: Arte Povera

1.

It's all impossible
the gesture impossible
the language impossible
the suture impossible:

a feather bead
                    kept in a useful bundle, with
                    one thing after another, mica, baby teeth,
                    satin fabric, weathered pebble, twine,
                    each layer wrapped and rapt.
                    A veritable vertigo of
                    "assemblages . . . "

2.

One and one and one make 111
by some calculi. Some tumuli.
Some cumulus or cumuli.
A house of clouds, its corridor
"shells, feathers, mirror, glass,
seaweed, sand and cut paper,"
opened onto a similarly
encrusted room.

3.

In the world as such
DNA dumplings
(with thin skin wrapped around them)
spatter recklessly
(unwittingly? uncannily?)

because of randomized events
in a politics of explosion.

How then?
Shaking with the instability
of calculations,
more in anger than in fear
one "shows one's work."

This is written entirely on off-cuts.
an internal translation of itself
marking shards with mackle.

It's true the work must be redone.
This time scribbling mirror-wise,
an addition(al) problem
with uncountable vectors.

4.

Suppose after all this, one just listed
house, book, mug, window,
daughter, dogs (gone), desk, Apple™.
Suppose it was budded tree limb, hair-thread fingers —
the baby oak in spring, rain "heavy at times,"
and the cleared branches of fall, suppose
yellow gusting in a greeny-pinkish light,
a dark red pear leaf blown into the room,
suppose a salvaged shmoo-like basil plant
eager, even in winter, to give pesto,
or a fondness, a warmth, eros
blue as the sky, could it be otherwise?
the apt healing of a wound, even with

[120]

its startling scar—
unaccountable enumerations:
the oddly glistening, the half-started language.
The half-startled. Twisting together
choice exemplars of exquisite debris:
"a cigar label, a metal buckle, a ballpoint pen,
a bottle cap, a bolt, a hair curler,
a drafting compass, a plastic bottle,
yellow tape, aluminum foil, drinking straws,
green paper,
broken blue glass."

5.

Would this be enough?
What would be enough?
It is never enough.

The task is unfinished,
the persons, unfinished.
The structure is unfinished.

Verso becomes a promise to turn back.

The sum total of "old furniture, planks and upside-down drawers,
cardboard cutouts,
scraps of insulation board, discarded light bulbs, jelly glasses, flower
vases, hollow cardboard cylinders, mirror fragments," with foil sheets
of gold and silver covering it all.

6.

When she had no canvas,
she took the wooden back
from a broken dresser drawer,

[121]

a board spotted, stained with dirt and with streaks
of paint jobs, color of the walls,
and painted a rag she saw hanging from the window
painted looking out from her window:
wall of brick and saturated rag hung limp,
the spots of grey, the grey spots on the board of the dresser
are now the snow falling, dirty, through the city.

7.

It's little things—a turquoise baby ring,
a shirt, upholstery tacks, cancelled stamps,
a box, a yellowing obit, and memories
of disasters of the past, or simply fountain pens,
or paper scraps with the writing
of the dead, or lists,
to speak of sheer lists,
that don't recognize
themselves as offering an outline
of rescue, of witness, and of care—
What can be done with them?

Part of the strangeness of writing,
the despair of it,
its ridiculous pretense,
and its nobility – is —
no song nor chime can be proposed
to animate regrets so small,
twisted and suffused
with our enormity.

The sound of this
is far more jagged, more like chunks:
"lilting Sprechstimme, synth dub interruptions,

howling tapecut-ups, and dust-bundles
of fuzz, static, and noise."
"You will know
that you will never know."

8.

Could list cloud-names
for the world's puff,
wisp, nacre and elegance,
moving above the world's implacable substance,
billowing over death, joy, rage,
lies, irreducible fractions
—over it all.
Poetry is not the goal.
The goal
is something smaller,
something more direct.
It doesn't seek for "poetry"
as overarching rubric name.

Wants simply to be present to itself,
neither to slide into astronomical despair,
nor into minutiae and only those,
("shirt collars, sample skeins
of embroidery thread,
rubber bands, shoelaces
and old darned socks"),
but still the stuff still shines.
It accumulates scintillation.
It is impossible to avoid
fractions of joy.

9.

Get all this down in time,
the collecting and sorting,
the car mirror smashed, the gusts of trash,
the candy wrappers on the street
bright with sweetish silvery-paper shine
against concrete.
And "metal, glass, neon, slate,
wax, earth & wood," facing
"air, wax, mirrors, lead,
newspaper, neon, pipe, and fabric" —
each mirroring each.

10.

Runnymede, Mnemosyne, a little brook
a little book, a little brucha,
a la-dee-da, a deed, you nested idioms
you vestiges, you remains,
these assemblages for
mixing things and words,
the ledges and ledgers,
the noman-dic measures
of sheer blessing,
the orange sun,
the storm/*orage*,
the orange moon:

you are instructed by the inner voice to
"bring all this with you into the silent room"

and also to carry a messier collect:
"scrap metal, off-cuts of wood,
broken machine parts, torn fabrics, buttons and coins."

11.

Mendicant
envoys

present themselves
as if prescient
about their own responsibility
to resist abandonment.
They will address
the imprint of our time:
interpreting its murky path
with the force of their postulates
about the unfinished.

We have an unreckonable fleshy pile
of the damages.
We have an unrecognizable fleshy pile
of the damages.
We have the cantata of anguishes,

"the enigmatic sigil of *more, for, there, now, without, not, if, already, save, who, I, when, neither, henceforth, he, beforehand, ah!, et cetera,* etc." and/ or "le sigle énigmatique de *plus, car, là, or, sans, pas, si, déjà, sauf, qui, je, quand, ni, désormais, il, auparavant, eh!, et caetera,* etc."

DECEMBER 2011–APRIL 2012

Draft 112: Verge

You know this story.

translation

First, "Horrible things happened
    and they were introduced to us
        as something good."   *something*
Killings.
    Uprootings.
        Fissures and divisions
between those
    who considered they were as   *splits*
        civic as the others,
or had more right to act, but
    at that punctual moment
        and then for years after,
found they were, or were found as, not.
    Certain atrocites   *borders*
        registered. Then were forgot.
Everyone, it seemed, had realigned,
    criss-crossed,
        double crossed.   *atrocities*
Maps had scratches, ridges, edges
    that they never before,
        it seemed, had.   *crossed*

Sizes, wires, assizes in the site, other boundaries on this border. Maps and line
are drawn over bodies. Where did "history" put this place? Why did it not "sta
there"? What about "them"? Should they live here, or are they basically foreign
What are the facts about myself? What is my where? It's true that once there wa
an ending. It seemed as if this were what I had wanted. Why did it then open?
hardly can remember, but then it's suddenly vivid, though even my own storie
have veered over time. Another time pulses through the stifled civic membrane

Restatement slid toward resentment.
    An otherwhere of once-upon-a-here   *passage*

took shape. Everyone
old incompatible stories.
   Everyone held to   *here*
      inconsolable memories.
veryone marked
   buried intensities of presence.
      Different and similar outcomes   *marked*
ere obliterated. Disappeared.
   Deemed incompatible.
      Altered.   *& buried*
oss became gain;
   gain compensated loss.
     It will remain, even if said, unsaid.

When the axe came into the forest, the trees thought, 'It's fine; that handle is
ne of us.'" What led to what? The incomparable, the scale off, the trans-located,
xiled, awkward and alarmed, the clatter, the shattering, have all been part of our
ves for so many years. This is what we have. Then you get tired. Then resigned.
hen it becomes half noticed. Or less. Where then, abruptly,

hereupon,
   many years later,
      people ask each visitor:
Have you crossed yet?" and say
   "You should."
      Meaning over to the other side.   *check-point*
hough there was no particular news,
   nothing to register except normal erosions,
      but the whole was considered   *normal*
omething to see.
   Shadows had already cast full sorts.
      And still they fell.

[127]

Everyone's insomnia is marked. Who wants to reflect on this? You might cur
insomnia by a very deep dream of sobbing. But that works for only one night. The
ordinary is so ironic: such as cascades of rusted metal trash water-falling down
the railroad cut. I mean where I do live. My eye core split and doubled. Now what
Sometimes things rest on mean-spirited technicalities. Cell phones do not work
across the divided city nor the nation(s); that is, you can't place a call down the
next block. Understanding and repairing were vague and then postponed. Ye
now a little has started. We may never know. That's all. Why should I say more?

"Who would kill an orange tree?"   *people*
    Sometimes anyone.
        It was a terrible way to be.
Here is her facing a life in
    the autobiography of a visage   *mirrored*
        written by alternative ears and eyes.
She does not match up
    with her doubled national flesh. Yet it looks like
        she filmed herself in a mirror. She filmed
herself as doppelgänger. She filmed as a mourner.   *other*
    A dialogic implacable crush
        of selves
sits shiva over the other   *selves*
    speaking on (or to)
        the crossroads of those shattered bits.
"What is man's relation
    to his/her own history?"
        said someone with a lexical-
rhetorical flourish
    of attempted fairness.
        This place,
as they said
    in the explanatory museum placard,
        is a "bone of content."

or there is a nano-second of resonance, of reverberating networks of sound that
indicate a meaning (or an illusion for a moment), even an oddity, beyond the
olly despair that might lead to nihilism if you simply "read the news." This nano-
ouch is called "the small." "The dot." "The person." Volta! Volta! Who can say
what this is to be in time, this strangest space, for there is something enormous
even inside the tiny spot of this smallish locale in which the thing called "I" (also
n-it-e, or me and it) cruises its happenstance. But then, to hammer in this point,
 heard of

hat man who would never cross
        (his wife told me this) because
                he refused to show his passport
t Border Control
        in what was (technically, for him)
                his "own country."

At the actual checkpoint,
        near the little maze and queue
                where people cross over   *line up*
arefully walking through,
        someone had graffito'd
                "No Borders"
s protest. So people read this   *identity card*
        on their way to the parallel ghetto
                in the other half-city.
When you got that twice-stamped visa
        like a high school hall pass signing you in
                and then out,
t came from a state
        that does not "officially exist."   *"homeland"*
                That itself means multiple things.
Questions: why, how, when, what and to whom.
        It was like living
                in a dream.

Which are the facts and which are the shadows? It is another knowledge of the country. "Don't try for peace (we HAVE peace). We want reconciliation." It was "a struggle between two historiographies . . .," someone noted. But it's clear that two were not enough. So "for starters," or "at least." Which is the door and which is the wall? Sometimes there is a sense of panic. One must record the sense of panic, the sense of grief, followed by the feeling of being snookered, lied to, manipulated. You have been honed by the chisel of it. Then became inured, numb. How much political irony can one person stand? "It's a textbook case." The Green Line became known by its other name: The Dead Zone.

Without her husband
    she crossed every week
        because certain groceries
were cheaper over there.
    She found
        streets that continued   *crossed*
the streets on her side
    ones she had always remembered,
        the small places being the same, or
pretty much, just slightly shabbier
    or maybe names changed to
        other heroic names,
but there was the wall blocking everything;   *cinder*
    there was scrub in between and sagging houses.
        Those too had names.   *blocks*

Because presumed temporary,
    the wall had been built shoddily
        and without any irony.
People's (long-ago mapped)
    houses and shops
        were now trapped.
The sealed, grim properties

had begun to look
            really terrible.

ttention: tourists/ visitors/ residents:
        you are forbidden
                snapshots.
JN Buffer Zone.
        No Photography.
            No Litter Please."

/here is one's own sense of what happened? Can one access one's own history
ith others? Articulate its stakes? There is shame on every level. Shame for every
de, and rage and shame for micro-twists of fractal sides. Twinned and tripled
ttaclysmic dreams bleed over all four margins down into the tight-sewn gutter
f the page. The book tries to contain and present these bloody verges. It fails. Bad
lood escapes.

he site was bolstered with sand bags,
        watchtowers, with strategic
            barrels filled with concrete   *description*
ıd a general double loopiness
        of barbed wire and razor wire
                built for business.
here it is: *cannot*
        The Border.
            Zagging and tacking thru the city,
ıbodied and embedded
        in unheimlich wandering.
            Despite the time that had gone by,   *convey*
ıe mix of boredom and menace
        that emanates from guns
                remains palpable.
ıt better not to seem
        to think too much

                    [131]

        or see too much
because the two acts
        and their auras as you walk
                might make you too visible.

Along the Dead Zone.   *it*
        can only run
                as fast as one can run.
Some things cannot be outrun.
        And sometimes
                where we are right now
those very things
        have all been done.
                Such times have taken place.

Cross-quarter day
        is halfway between solstices,
                and just between solaces.
One throw of the dict
        did not annulify
                the chunk of fate,
nor definitional geographies of Treaties
        nor hierarchies of Passports,
                nor pious Conspiracies of Certitude.

Corners once protected
        from sniper fire
                where armed men
had hidden in concrete boxes and peered out
        are now dirtied excrescences
                surrounded by dried grass.
Twenty different brands of trashed
        water bottles thrown into the Zone   *zone*
                cannot be cleaned up

because entering the scrub-between
      could still get you shot.
            So it's garbage-y
right through.
      Like a vacant lot.
               Never mind
the level of forgetting
      and those condemned to remember,
            nor strains of verb and noun
between forgetting
      and remembering.
            Each was on the verge of shifting over.   *verge*
One side saw the Dead Zone
      as temporary,
            the other as permanent.
But the sides kept changing
      which was which.
            The stakes were such
that no one knew
      how to calibrate all this.
            To say
"reunify" was sometimes close.
      Though people remain at odds   *damages*
            over sovereignty, alliances,
and control
      ("of the military").
            There's also the contentious
writing of public history,
      ("school books"); there's
            restitution or not
of houses and gardens that others
      have lived in, fondly, planting,
            weeding, making them their
very own for fifty-plus years.

[133]

How to calculate?
        "Private Property?"
  "Reparations?"   *"orange trees"*

The cost involved the cost of words. There was also the question of which language, or both. Or yet another language—English. Like a fairy tale, this ques demanded the tracking of paths, where all signatory phosphorescence had faded and where the signs were often broken, left like shards. Is there a residue tha remains? Mend? or sweep away? This poises on the sedimentation of micro-tones on empathy for dark news read in the darkness with listening eyes, and with ear all inky, smudged by little shaking hands. Thanatos might take care of itself. It' desire that needs nurturing. "Change or Die TPYING." The P is Greek for how w would write R.

DECEMBER 2011–APRIL 201

Draft 113: Index

Words become heated up as if they were to start to glow again in the disenchanted world, as if the promise hidden in them had become the motor of thought.

ADORNO, *"Ernst Bloch's Spuren [Traces]."*

```
ERROR: syntaxerror
OFFENDING COMMAND:  — nostringval—
STACK:
false
-mark-
false
-mark-
/OtherSubrs
-dictionary-
/Private
-dictionary-
-dictionary-
```

HP Laserjet 1200 *Series, personal communication,* 2011

A
    see not-A
    see also The
Abraham
Abyss
Accidentals
Adorno, Theodor
Age of Ash
    see also long 20th
    Century
Aiglio
Air
Alphabet
"Andante con Scratchy"
Angel
    see Jacob
    see Stranger, Ladder
Answerlessness

Aphorism
Apple
Archive
As if
Astonishment
Avant-texte
Awkwardness
Azure
    password, thread, sky

Babel
Bad Dog
Bees
Benjamin, Walter
Between
Birds, various simple varieties
Bits
Black Hole

[136]

Grit
Gusts

H (aitch, acca, aspirated, etc.)
Haibun
H.D.
Headlines
Hecatomb
Hinges
Hole
Hope
Horizon
How
      many
      much
      dare me!
Huh!
Human Sacrifice
Hungry

Identify
      empathy
      taxonomy
Incipience
Index
Inside
Instrumentality
Inter-related
Interstices
Intertwined
Investigation
Is
Isaac
It

Jealousy
Job Lot
Jots
Journal
Journey
Joy
Juncture
Justice

Kinwing
Klezmer
Knife
      & bushy outcrop in
      which something is
      hidden — sharpened
      intransigence
Knot
Known
        un-

Labor
Labyrinth
Lapis Lazuli
Lede
Letter
      see Alphabet
Lexicon
Light
Limen
Listen
Lists
Little
Livre

paper
    metal
Scroll
Seely
Selvedge
Sentence
Shadow
Shakiness
Sheep,
       as in "heigh ho silly"
Shim
Shoah
Shoelaces
Signage
Silence
Silver
Skepticism
Smudge
Snakes
"Socio-twistiness"
Space
Spindle
Spring
     source
     printemps
     <u>*and All*</u>
Stranger
Stars
Stein, Gertrude
String Quartet
Stone
    see also Pebble
Struggle
Swerve

Syntax

Talismanic
Talmudic (metaphoric, secular
    use only)
Task
Telos
Tenso
Tertium Quid
Textile
The
Theory, see Practice
There
Threads
Tilt
Times New Roman
Tin Tea Trunk (aka doll suitcase)
Title
To Be
     essere
     stare
Toll
Toywort
Trace
™
Train
Translation
Trees, see also branches, roots,
    leaves,   seeds, fruit,
   social life of
Tristram Shandy
Triumphalist
     see anti-triumphalist
Tsuris

Tunnel
Turquoise
Twirls

Ultima Thule
Umbria
Universe, the
Unsayable, the
Ur-
Useful Knots and how to tie
    them
Ut

Valises
Vectors
Verge
Vertigo
    see also dizziness
Vestiges
Vigil
Void
Volcano
Volta (i.e. Turn)
Volume
        sound
        space
        tome

Walks
Wandering chorus
Watch
        tell time
        attend, register
Water

Wayward
Webbing
Weslowski (see Weslock)
Why
Wide
Wireman, The Philadelphia
Woof
        see also Warp
Woolf, Virginia
Word
Work
        see work, work, work

X
        as in crossing, as in
        cross-outs,
        as in crossroads

Y.
Yeast
Yes
Yod
        see also Yid, Yad
Youse

Zimzum
Zone
        Apollinaire (Q.V.)
        encirclement (girdle,
        obs.)
        space
        time
Zukofsky, Louis, oh yes,
        Zukofsky,

Zuzzurellona

2009–2011

Draft 114: Exergue and Volta

It's how to finish and how
to begin again,
it's always the same
dilemma (again),
yet always shifting.

It's how to read
works haptic as a nest of quipu
where strung knots twist
their tangled fullness,
changing over into under,
under to over.

Yet being on this endge
changes almost nothing.
Is that so surprising?
The texts are apparitions,
haunted by themselves,
ghosting the writer,
whereever she now
is.

*And I when I got willing to stop anywhere, though for years fairly in mind had
been the idea and aim of long as possible works about like the desire to live for
good or have a good (various?) thing never end, then like walking down the
street noticing things a poem would extend itself.*

~

No matter what—
the awe of the mark
petrifies.
That risk is a magnet
for hard iron shapes.

For the horizon.
For inchoate intensities.
For the unknown.

There's fear of creating
corny satisfactions
from petty thinking—
one's distaste
for half-measures
and self-delusions.

Yet once the hands grasp
at the alphabet
and tap related glyphs
(ex.: & and —),
arrives excess,
plethora and possibility.
Then there is awe and fear of that,
of being awash
or flooded out.

From nothing to everything,
from desiccation to drowning:
this
is the tidal surge of writing.
This is the way it is; how can it
stop?

Ordinarily anybody finishes anything.
But not in writing. In writing not any one finishes anything. [. . .]
Please act as if there were the finishing of anything but any one any one writ-
ing knows that there is no finishing finishing in writing.

Here is the book, and here is its shadow.
Sentenced to sentences.
Such constant metamorphoses—
dark to light, white bits pulsing
through capillaries
threaded around inky blackness,
the luminosity, intermittence, ruin
imprinted here as historical air
become
hard to encompass.

Actually,
impassible.

Entering the book of the unraveling voice
while slightly panicked, slightly rushed,
working distressed ends of multiple strands—
this never was to be a scintillating ball
(a crystal rounded, shaped and somewhat turgid)
nor was it one singularity
twisting brilliantly through its self-made maze.
Instead it became a (fat) (impassable) shadow.

Speak of complexity!
Speak of closing via opening!
Speak of the oddness of
it.

And the poem itself chooses to be disordered (in many senses) so there really isn't
a "beginning" and "end." [Later: this isn't right. Yes, there's a beginning and
end, but there's also a sense in which it's ongoing, doesn't reach a conclusion,
or does so only tentatively: "all this writing never thinks of having an end — ."]

Pulse, pulse, pulse—
that forward drive of statement.
Which thinking necessitates,
which writing requires.
A book is thus like time.

Perhaps this pulse
also demands closure?
To give the satisfactions
of delight, it must conclude
in ways we have been led to like.

A book will rule its pleasure
because it will resolve—
reveal some mystery.

And it will also
revel and roil in itself,
questioning
how we got here
and where it is we
are.

Thereupon it will resolve, yes,
stubbornly to begin once more.
Resolve to re-assess
yet not repeat,
reordering its wayward line.
A book therefore
is not like time;
one can go differently,
reread, remember,

pursue another pleasure.
Frottage, fricage, penetration, touching.

Any book is paradoxical—pulsing across
—down—into the passage of time
on the page
while lavish with recursive
surging
inside the turn and charge of
words.

*. . . one might find stopping, concluding, settling, giving up, ending, solution,
and perhaps even opening, beginning again (and again). And if everything is
perpetually beginning again and again, it is also finishing again and again, but
once everything is finishing again and again, finishing is simply another version
of beginning.*

~

The sound comes from inside
the body, from the whorl of ears

as if the bumps of the brain opened
inside out to make those ears

as if the bumps of the joints
and the sexes opened happily

turning in other directions
folding fresh to the air

making ears be echo chambers
of their own originality

[148]

and the originality of others,
while tunneling backwards

black dot, black page,
black hole.

A book of continuations not of conclusions, I build even as I prepare the book for the publisher at last, living once more as I copy, and take over wherever I see a new possibility in the work.

∿

Intensify doing
Shatter doing
Intensify the shattered
It does not rest there;
it will rest
nowhere.

Over the headlands
views, bluffs, trails.
Two layers of clouds
one, briefly, stable,
another veiled and blowing
swift skimming scrim,
the pattern curdled, stirring milk
into water, a grey-scale blur,
a congestion of changing colors—
these folds and pleats.

Therefore L. asked
"can you think of something
neither the codex or the scroll?"
Well, the box.

"Can you think outside the box?"
The plinth or tombstone.
The so-called "infinite" extensions of hypertext.
The sand mandala,
color-shapes precise and exacting,
then jumbled, destroyed,
rainbows pushed together,
thrown with joy
into the flowing water.

The gloss of another text upon the text,
and one upon that
riding the eros of
pli upon pli,
to rive the book,
to rouse the book,
scattering its

possibilities,

a reopening of closure.

∽

"Writing is neither
remembering nor forgetting
neither beginning or ending."
Huh. Writing is remembering
and forgetting; it is
beginning *and* ending;
it is all of the above *and* more—
all occurring—let loose—
in non-sequential,
interlaced, intensifying order.

As for the georgic or other erg-ish formation—
it is heterogeneous information
about work processes.
The coin is stamped.
This is its other side,
an exergue,
the mark of place and time.
Umbria, August 2012 and prior,
Philadelphia, December 2011 and prior,
a bit of Durham, N.C., a wee touch
of Auckland, N.Z. Plausible?
Privileged? Peripatetic? Exilic?
This die is cast as such.

The place has varied;
the time is always now,
or no; it is now and then,
or not and them,
or nor and than;
the text itself
is the ever-ready secret.

My right eye
tears in the painful, gritty wind
of what it reads
and what it sees.
There is
no further
secret.

But it was not the end.

Form is passion.

~

Our alphabet will always end its little charm with

Z

Over again this sing-song tune is sung.

I want a juicy black pen,
to help me out here
help me out of here
a-tumble
down the lossening zig-zag track
of time.

En route! Something
is foundational, something reckless
something desired.
So register that swirled flashed
     flicker-emanation
          of accumulated restlessness.
How to calibrate?
     Sometimes the obvious,
         but filled with strangeness.

Words being epistles of sounding, of
soundings. The future of
future at the present time.
There is no "ending" exactly
but maybe processes,

countless diversified nuances.

～

This next bit could be the end
(you think?):
The level of resistance was so high
it used up four N-shaped mountains
before it ever got to Y.
Were there enough options?
Not even.

"Poetry is hyper-saturated
because of the multiplicity of
filiated, but (paradoxically) not
completely speakable impacts."

Overload, again,
simply of
the commonplace.
Of what is.
Plus what is dreamed —
my gathering up
the scattered teardrops,
field of crystals
on the ground.

Are we bombing or feeding?
Am I beginning or ending?
The whole white diagnosis of mist
between the snow-laden sky
and the sleet slick sidewalk
of beginnings, I mean —
do I mean endings?

closure is an inevitability of anything you can identify as an act a   performance

or even a process   because the tendency of a process is to play itself out in a
certain direction and either to arrive at an ending or imply one as you walk
away from it   so even if you walk away from it   it still feels closed

≈

And Look at it!
So much slippage!
How many words and torquing shapes
        can be made, or could depend
        from this variety of thickly imperfect
Findings.
Performances. Whatever.
I work in paper, found objects, syntax, lexicons and glue.
I draw from historical and personal happenstance
to create information not
called that. Also attention-getting
spume of slap and tide, black sand,
gold sand and pelican thrust
pierce along
with wildy waves and deepish foam
luscious with presences.

(Should I be worried
about the *"aesthetics of lusciousness"*?)

This is just the piano reduction.
If you could only hear
the symphony! If I could only
conduct it! Or write it!
Electricity.
Flat out from the flash.

Who can say

what it is to be in time
or any other strangest dangerous
place?

The book is always other, it changes and is exchanged by comparing the diver-
sity of its parts, and thus we avoid the linear movement — the one-way direc-
tion — of reading. Moreover, the book, unfolded and refolded, scattering and
being gathered back together, shows that it has no substantial reality: it is never
there, endlessly to be unmade while it is made.

∾

Y should end it, no? or yes.
Some symmetry of no and yes.
Or even a greater NO.
Etc. But.
Why should I end it?
I toast our knobby, inexplicable joy,
the surge in the discursive system
with saturated colors and low-grade special effects.

There is plethora
in the vastness of the words
for worlds
and the little in it,
in that word
central to text—
barashit—
which means *a* beginning,
one or another beginning,
in something translated
as "The Beginning."

Mon page was mis à nu.

Mites work the world.
One ant sharp as a black letter
front fore-legs held up high
strong as an ox
(proportionately speaking)
carries a seed sac
ten times longer, heavier than it is.
It heaves unevenly down its particular path.

Perfection is dispersed,
it is
its own answerlessness
made of smallish, suspicious,
semi-inarticulate,
totally inadequate
responses, masquerading,
mockingly,
as sufficient. And trying
for a kind of "beauty" in accuracy.

Something like that.
Sometimes they were
actually called "answers,"
but they were not,
and no one believed this
much
but they were the outcomes of
honesty
observation
analysis
languages
and
a haunted hungering.
It is worth considering for a moment the notion of ends. The word has numer-

ous connotations: withering, eclipse; fullness; closure, termination, catastro-
phe, death; turning or stopping points; goals and targets. It summons an array
of phenomena: finitude, beginnings and middles, expected change, nostalgia,
mourning. It suggests remains, revenants, immortality.

∽

N ways to say
    darkening brightness;
  to say in R there was Redness.
in Y there were questions.
    in X there were Cross-roads,
in A there were Rocks.
Ahoy
Writing was growing along the margins of the sky
and swift down the watershed ruck
and then
the air will blow and obscure what was written
and then
writing will be encased in upthrust shoals
like white intrusions in black rock,
necessitating
continuous charges of worded-thinking—
electric, scintillating,
even risky—with any luck.

Did I cite?
Did I say?
twisted together
Edge-fold wanderer.

The text expands the letter
the letter implodes in the text
way blazed as randonné

if you can read the blazes
(or maybe you get lost).
The very clarities of quartz
are filled with smoke lines, shimmering
but also a *giallo*, a thriller, body parts wandering,
fear, darkened bleeding, congealed suspicion,
reloaded staircases, unassuageable
sadness, resisted webbings,
spiders nesting in the house.

We read the little bumps and sounds these leave
caught randomly, transparent ribbons—
little strips blowing towards each other—
shining luminous banners in the darkening copse.

So a *"leaving (without ending)"*
acknowledging
"the idea of departure"
without actually leaving . . .

$$\sim$$

What is outside this book?
That person wrote her exam
with a dogged inattention:
"this poem has a revolution at the end."
We should be so fortunate—
or, actually, maybe not.
Was it resolution she meant to say?
Or revelation?

"Now my own suspicion is that the Universe is not only queerer
than we suppose, but queerer than we can suppose."

[158]

Thus *"no last word"*

∿

That this began
that this ends
that this refused to begin
(though it started)
that it refuses to end
(though it is folding itself up)

We offer a full spectrum of services
going round

"into an imagined 'endlessness'"
endlessly overwritten.

The page is stamped in saturated black
in which

the last lines herein placed
are thus unreadable
hidden within a glossy square of ink:
it is
finished but it is
not complete.
Is black all colors?
Or was that white?
"I am not sure that is not the end"

so that . . . .
or simply *"So . . . "*
going backwards
through the work's own vibrato,

it's 4:32 AM exactly
in the wind that's blowing fiercely.
There are so many tasks. To start.

Up. Again.

Like this. The is, the it.

Id est:

So vector the crossroads once again!
Volta! Volta!

2008–2012

Notes to Drafts 96–114

Notes to Draft 96: Velocity. It was the Old World or Common Yellow Swallowtail—*Papilio machaon*. *Parnassius mnemosyne*, also a swallowtail, is both rarer and endangered. The citation in German is from Rilke, from the first Duino Elegy. "We're coming here with pieces of people we lost," stated by Norma Gabriel Taylor and cited by Matt Saldaña in an article about the first inauguration of Barack Obama, *The Independent: The Triangle's Weekly*, Jan. 22, 2009, 5. The poem is the first work of beginning again on the "line of one."

There are no notes to Draft 97.

Notes to Draft 98: Canzone. The citation: "The bit of ugly, the glitch, the torn, the sweeper, the tender, the constant reminder that things are being unmade and tended" is by Sina Queyras, 9 May 2009, on Jeff Wall, photographer, taken from her Lemon Hound blog. Draft on the "line of three."

Notes to Draft 99: Intransitive. This poem was written just after the death of Robin Blaser, May 7, 2009. Walt Whitman, "Crossing Brooklyn Ferry" is the source of the material in italics. "Everything in it is both head and tail alternately reciprocally" is cited from Ron Silliman's blog of 12 May 2009 and is his citation of a letter from Charles Baudelaire to Arsène Houssaye, serving as the introduction to *Paris Spleen*. The poet as frog is the "Portrait of Ono no do fu composing a poem," Japanese, c. 1530, in the Barnes Collection, Philadelphia. "In this section there is much crossing of hands," is from program notes by John Corigliano for his "Etude Fantasy," 1976. "Displays of mental confusions with intrusions of irrelevant information(s)." Said by Marlene Dumas, as a self-descriptor of her work, slightly modified, from the information sheet for Miss Interpreted, her show at Philadelphia's Institute of Contemporary Art, December 1993. Some film terms, loosely speaking, from Carol Clover in conversation. Poem is on the "line of four."

Notes to Draft 100: Gap. The Walter Benjamin citation in the poem is the sentence engraved in German, Catalan, Spanish, and English on the monument in Port Bou, Spain made by sculptor Dani Karavan and called "Passages: Homage to Walter Benjamin." The sentence that follows is "Historical construction is devoted to the memory of the nameless." From Benjamin's "On the Concept of History." Draft along the "line of 5."

There are no notes to Draft 101.

Notes to Draft 102: One-on-One. "Double fault with precarious vessels" is the title of a sculpture by Paula Winokur. This "idiosyncretismic weigh" was said to me by Peter Quartermain in an email, characterizing *Drafts*. Draft 102 is on the line of seven.

Notes to Draft 103: Punctum. The concept of the "punctum" derives from Roland Barthes, *Camera Lucida*; the epigraph is from p. 96. Gray's "Elegy" lies somewhere behind the generation of this poem. The prose of section 1, with thanks to Erín Moure. The citation beginning "The reader will find . . . " is from student Donovan Tann. "The living hand" is, of course, Keats. The eclipse occurred in early 2007, over Lake Como. This draft is on the "line of 8."

There are no notes to Draft 104.

Note to Draft 105: Pilgrimage. The small raptor was probably an immature Sharp-shinned Hawk (Accipiter striatus).

Notes to Draft 106: Words. The fifth line from the end is taken directly and modified from an epigram that Orhan Pamuck attributes to Ibn Zerhani in *The Black Book* (Chapter Two): "Nothing can ever be as shocking as life. Except writing." My response to Wittgenstein follows. Of course, I could be naïve—everything depends on what he means by "the case."

Notes to Draft 107: Meant to say. The epigraph from P. Inman, stated during his *Philly Talks* in 1999. Photojournalist David Swanson answers the question "Looking back what did you learn in Iraq?" posed by Steve Volk in "View to a Kill," *Philadelphia Weekly*, March 9–15, 2005: 11–12. The last lines come from my mini-poem for a Dusie "wee book." Draft 107 is on the "line of 12."

Notes to Draft 108: Ballad and Gloss. The artist Sidney Goodman was the former owner of the house we own now. Wikipedia was useful on the subject of "oranges," and *The New York Times* Science section for other materials. Source of the material about histones as a passive spool vs. active framework from *NYTimes Science*, Feb. 24, 2009, by line, Nicholas Wade; headline "From One Genome, Many Types of Cells. But How?" p. D4.This poem is on the "line of 13."

Notes to Draft 109: Wall Newspaper. As shadow epigraph: "These poems and this poet continue the recognitions of the other poet and his poems." Robin Blaser on Jack Spicer's *Lorca Poems*. "The Practice of Outside," *The Fire: Collected Essays of Robin Blaser*, ed. Miriam Nichols. Berkeley: University of California Press, 2006, 144.

Section I: Of the Dead.
March 2011: Fukushima, Japan, 9.0 earthquake, tsunami, and subsequent meltdown and leakage from nuclear reactors run by TEPCO: Tokyo Electric Power Company. (In 2012, a report issued by the Fukushima

[162]

Nuclear Accident Independent Investigation Commission concluded that the disaster was preventable, "rooted in government-industry collusion and the worst conformist conventions of Japanese culture" [*International Herald Tribune*, July 6, 2012].) Other extreme weather events are present — like the several tornadoes in the United States during 2011 and the 2004 earthquake in Haiti. And other ecological disasters caused by malfeasance — such as the BP Gulf of Mexico oil spill. "Mann geboren frei ist," a German translation of the first phrase of Jean-Jacques Rousseau's *Social Contract* (1762)."Stony rubbish" along with a few unmarked phrases throughout: T.S. Eliot, "The Waste Land." "Nature suddenly appeared like an emptied room." Wilfred Wiegand, June 19, 2001, now not sure of the source.

"Of odds and ends in constant flux manipulated by desire and fear," T.S. Eliot, *Nation and Athenaeum* on Donne, 1923."Being "born," as Olson said, "not of the buried but these unburied dead," Charles Olson, "La Préface." R. M. Rilke: You must change your life: "Du musst dein Leben ändern" ("Archaic Torso of Apollo"). "Replete with signifiers and gibberish" (a former student). Chaos Becomes a Way of Life, *NYTimes* headline re. Haitian earthquake and its aftermath, Feb 16, 2004. by line Lydia Polgreen (front page). Eating wood — fact from Seurasaari Open-Air Museum outside of Helsinki, Finland. "Dominant, residual, and emergent" are terms from Raymond Williams, characterizing simultaneous and interactive social formations, in *Marxism and Literature*. "The word" she said "leads inward into itself," Susan Handelman, *The Slayers of Moses: The Emergence of Rabbinic Interpretation in Modern Literary Theory*, 1982, 31.

Section II: Gamut
"A little doll is the solution." (a now untrackable citation). "The unspeakable words never cease their subversive action," Nicolas Abraham and Maria Torok, *The Shell and the Kernel: Renewals of Psychoanalysis*, 1994, 132. The composer Stefan Wolpe spoke of Zweiheimigkeit as well as "labyrinths of terrible differences," taken from Brigid Cohen's article about his political work in music, *Berlin Journal* 19 (Fall 2010): 36–39 *www.americanacademy.de/ uploads/media/BJ19_web.pdf*
"I hold my honey and I store my bread. . . . " Gwendolyn Brooks, from "Gay Chaps at the Bar," the sonnet "my dreams my works, must wait till after hell." *Selected Poems*, 1963, 23. The forgotten woman artist whom my friend mentioned is Jean Follett, actually.

Section III: Fire Surf
"We have our marching orders. We will be playing the killed civilians," Slobodan Simic, Serb aphorist, *NYTimes* 2 Dec 2007, modified. "As they exit, they strike an antique cymbal, which reverberates in unison with the cello harmonic." George Crumb, about "Night of the Four Moons" [1969], his composition to texts by Frederico Garcia Lorca. "He etches the places you are not supposed to notice" — the work of printmaker Amze Emmons. The citation "And O/   the voices of the children,/ singing in the dome

above" is from Robert Duncan's "Parsifal (After Wagner and Verlaine)" in *Bending the Bow*, 57, translating a line from T.S. Eliot's "The Waste Land," "Et O ces voix d'enfants, chantant dans la coupole," line 202 of "The Fire Sermon," itself being the final line of Paul Verlaine's sonnet "Parsifal." The next lines from Stephen Collis: "We were anxious about the market of everything/ About the sound of our voices in the cavernous dome" from "Let me Speak Clearly" in *On The Material*, Talonbooks, 2010, 14.

Section V. Thunderstorm Dawn
"My writing is a kind of American that *talented* cats and dogs could read," John Ashbery, riffing on a line from Marianne Moore's poem "England": "plain American which cats and dogs can read." Ashbery in an interview with Michael Glover published in *The New Statesman*, 23 May 2005. "You see, I look at my paintings, speculate about them. They baffle me, too. That's all I'm painting for." Philip Guston, at the University of Minnesota, March 1978. The citation "There was a brief break before the beating . . .," Dorothy Parvas, journalist for *Al Jazeera*, about her being held in detention in Syrian prisons, from the important account that she wrote after her release, May 2011.

"Voyage autour de mes cartes postales" is the title of a poem by James Schuyler. The sentence beginning "Of metamorphosis . . . " is a muted citation from my note on the Marianne Moore plaque at the New York Public Library. *PMLA* 126.1 (January 2011): 20–21. "I would like to be able to write a book that is only an Incipit" from Italo Calvino, *If on a Winter's Night a Traveler*. Trans. William Weaver, 1981,177. "Discovering new ways of folding," Gilles Deleuze, *The Fold* 1988/1993, 137. "This rrrr   to be a river," Robert Duncan, *Bending the Bow*, "The Collage, Passages 6," 20. "Rien n'aura eu lieu   que le lieu" (Nothing has taken place except the place). Stéphane Mallarmé, *Un Coup de Dés*. "She carries a book/of the unwritten volume" modified from H.D. *Trilogy*. "Wer, wenn ich schriee, hörte mich denn. . . . " is the first line of Rainer Maria Rilke, *Duino Elegies*, I. (literally: Who, were I to cry out, would then hear me. . . .) "We have constructed ruins/ to be reborn out of," Lorenzo Thomas, "Like a Tree," *Dancing on Main Street*, Coffee House Press, 2004.

Notes to Draft CX: Primer. The whole visual-poetic work is in *The Collage Poems of Drafts* in color. Only the "Preface" is reprinted in this book.

Notes to Draft 111: Arte Povera. Section 1. The full citation is "Her assemblages are constructed of both found and fabricated materials, ranging from lockers, cupboards, and wineglasses to plywood and knitted wire." Dorothy Cross, *Power House*, Philadelphia ICA exhibit, 1991. One word remains. Section 2. Brochure for A La Ronde, House of Shells, A 376 in the direction of Exmouth, South-east of Exeter, England. Section 3. "Internal translation," a concept from Hölderlin, noted by Philippe Lacoue-Labarthe, *Heidegger and the Politics of Poetry*, trans. Jeff Fort (Champaign: University of Illinois Press, 2007), 69. Section 4. The "shmoo" is an amiable creature created by Al Capp in his *L'il Abner* comic strip. List of some of the many Wireman objects (slightly reorganized) from Brendan Greaves, "Bare Wires" in Philadelphia Wireman catalog, Fleisher/Ollman Gallery, 2011. Section 5. Smithsonian Museum of American Art's description (slightly cut) of the materials in James Hampton's ca. 1950–64 work *The Throne of the Third Heaven of the Nations' Millennium General Assembly*, Washington D.C. Section 6. The artist mentioned is Alice Neal. Section 7. The "lilting Sprechstimme . . .," by John Corbett on David Grubbs—found in my folder for Draft 35: Verso, but have no idea where it comes from. There is also a citation from Maurice Blanchot, *Writing the Disaster*, 82. Section 8. "Shirt collars . . .," part of the list of Sheila Hicks's materials; Joan Simon, from Simon and Susan Faxton, *Sheila Hicks: 50 Years*, New Haven: Yale University Press, 2010, 112. Section 9. "Metal, glass . . .," Tate Modern description on internet of *Zero to Infinity, Arte Povera 1962–1972*; "air, wax, mirrors . . .," Walker Art Gallery description of materials in the same show. Section 10. From a Quaker pamphlet found at Briggflatts. And "scrap metal . . . " from Roger Cardinal and Gwendolen Webster, *Kurt Schwitters, Kurt Schwitters: A Journey Through Art* (Ostfildern, Germany: Hatje Cantz, 2011), 39. Section 11. "the enigmatic sigil . . . " and "le sigle énigmatique . . .," Jacques Derrida, *Signéponge/ Signsponge,* trans. Richard Rand, (New York: Columbia University Press, 1984, 118–119. This poem is on the "line of 16."

Notes to Draft 112: Verge. The poem cites from Yiannis Papadakis, *Echoes from the Dead Zone: Across the Cyprus Divide*. London: I.B. Tauris & Co Ltd, 2005. Quotations from his work are italicized. There are also two citations in quotation marks (what I heard and wrote down) from the video by Kutlug Ataman, "1+1=1," 2002, concerning Cyprus, and seen in the Istanbul Modern Museum in 2011. A description and extension of her work also occurs. A further push came from Mary Layoun, *Wedded to the Land? Gender, Boundaries, and Nationalism in Crisis*. Durham: Duke University Press, 2001; I cite a proverb she also cited. The "bone of content" is a phase I actually found on a museum placard. This poem also draws on a few comments made about a work by the Belgian artist Francis Alÿs. In 2004, Alÿs walked along the armistice border in Jerusalem, also known as "the green line." Alÿs used green paint to mark his démarche. See *Sometimes Doing Something Poetic Can Become Political And Sometimes Doing Something Political Can Become Poetic: The Green Line, Jerusalem* 2004–2005 (New York: David Zwirner, s.d.). Donor drafts are 17, 36, 55, 74, and 93, that is: Unnamed, Cento, Quiptych, Wanderer and Romantic Fragment Poem.

Notes to Draft 113: Index.
The first epigraph comes from Theodor Adorno, "Ernst Bloch's Spuren [Traces]." *Essays*, vol. I, 204. The second epigraph is an autonomously printed communication from my HP Laserjet 1200 Series, sending me a little back-talk, 2011. The "Andante con Scratchy" is in Charles Ives, Second String Quartet. This poem is on the "line of 18."

Notes to Draft 114: Exergue and Volta.

Citation, first section

"And I when I got willing to stop anywhere, though for years fairly in
mind had been the idea and aim of long as possible works about like
the desire to live for good or have a good (various?) thing never end,
then like walking down the street noticing things a poem would
extend   itself." Larry Eigner, "Approaching things: Some Calculus
How figure it Of Everyday Life Experience." *The L=A=N=G=U=A=G=E Book*,
ed. Bruce Andrews and Charles Bernstein, Southern Illinois University
Press, 1984, 3.

Citation, second section

    "Ordinarily anybody finishes anything.
    But not in writing. In writing not any one finishes anything. That is what
makes a master-piece what it is that there is no finishing.
    Please act as if there were the finishing of anything but any one any one
writing knows that there is no finishing finishing in writing." Gertrude
Stein. *The Geographical History of America or the Relation of Human Nature to the
Human Mind.* Johns Hopkins University Press, [1936] 1973, 222.

Citations, third section

'And the poem itself chooses to be disordered (in many senses) so there
really isn't a "beginning" and "end." [Later: this isn't right. Yes, there's a
beginning and end, but there's also a sense in which it's ongoing, doesn't
reach a conclusion, or does so only tentatively: "all this writing never
thinks of having an end —."]' The internal citation is by George Stanley;
the statement as a whole from Beverly Dahlen, "Some notes on George
Stanley's *Vancouver: A Poem*"
http://jacketmagazine.com/37/stanley-by-dahlen.shtml

Citations, fourth section

"Fricage" — a word learned from Kate Lilley's note to her poem "Starry
Messenger" in *Versary* (Salt Publishing, 2002), an early modern word
denoting acts of a lewd (lesbian) woman.
'Perhaps one might even say that during the last pages of a long poem one
might find stopping, concluding, settling, giving up, ending, solution,
and perhaps even opening, beginning again (and again)." Rachel Blau
DuPlessis, *Blue Studios: Poetry and Its Cultural Work.* University of Alabama
Press, 2006, 246. With the addition of other writing by me (from the
revised "Woolfenstein a sequel," 2012).

Citation, fifth section

" . . . a book of continuations not of conclusions, I build even as I prepare the
book for the publisher at last, living once more as I copy, and take over
wherever I see a new possibility in the work." Robert Duncan, *The H.D.
Book*, University of California Press, 2011, 427.

Citations, sixth section

L. is Alan Loney in his aphoristic meditations on the book. *The books to come.*

Victoria, TX: Cuneiform Press, 2010. A paraphrase of his argument on 70–71.

"a reopening of closure" is the title of a book by Murray Krieger, published by Columbia University Press in 1989.

Citations, seventh section
"Writing is neither remembering nor forgetting neither beginning or ending." Gertrude Stein, line of *The Geographical History of America or the Relation of Human Nature to the Human Mind*. Johns Hopkins University Press, [1936] 1973, 142.

"Form is passion." Ron Silliman, *The Alphabet* [from *Demo*]. University of Alabama Press, 2008, 23.

Citation, eighth section
" . . . by choosing more concrete, more phenomenologically exact inceptions, we shall come to realize that the dialectics of inside and outside multiply with countless diversified nuances." This was said in the course of an argument against binarist thinking. Gaston Bachelard, *The Poetics of Space*. Trans. Maria Jolas. Boston: Beacon Press, 1994, 216.

Citations, ninth section
This section contains a self-citation from my essay on Zukofsky's handbook of poetry and poetics, "*A Test of Poetry* and Conviction," from the 2004 Louis Zukofsky Centennial Conference. *Jacket Magazine. http://jacketmagazine. com/30/index.shtml*

"closure is an inevitability of anything you can identify as an act a performance or even a process   because the tendency of a process is to play itself out in a certain direction and either to arrive at an ending or imply one as you walk away from it   so even if you walk away from it   it still feels closed"

but it "is not so much the manner of ending but the scale . . . . .a work of great magnitude cant have a lot in common with a work [the sonnet is his example] that is easily encompassed in a much smaller scale." David Antin, *John Cage Uncaged is still Cagey*. San Diego: Singing Horse Press, 2005, 69.

Citations, tenth section
"aesthetics of lusciousness." Ron Silliman, *The Grand Piano: An Experiment in Collective Autobiography, Part* 9. This Press, 84.

"The book is always other, it changes and is exchanged by comparing the diversity of its parts, and thus we avoid the linear movement — the one-way direction — of reading. Moreover, the book, unfolded and refolded, scattering and being gathered back together, shows that it has no substantial reality: it is never there, endlessly to be unmade while it is made." Maurice Blanchot, *The Book to Come*. Trans. Charlotte Mandell. Stanford University Press, 2003, 266.

Citations, eleventh section
Hank Lazer discussed the ambiguity of the Hebrew word *barashit* in comments made at a panel in which we both participated.

"It is worth considering for a moment the notion of *ends*. The word has numerous connotations: withering, eclipse; fullness; closure, termination, catastrophe, death; turning or stopping points; goals and targets. It summons an array of phenomena: finitude, beginnings and middles, expected change, nostalgia, mourning. It suggests remains, revenants, immortality." Vincent B. Leitch, "Theory Ends." *Profession* 2005: 122–128. Citation on 124.

Citation, twelfth section
"leaving (without ending)" and "the idea of *departure*": Barbara Guest, *Quill Solitary APPARITION*, The Post-Apollo Press, 1996, 50, 49.

Citations, thirteenth section
"Now my own suspicion is that the Universe is not only queerer than we suppose, but queerer than we can suppose." J.B. S. Haldane, *Possible Worlds and Other Papers* (1927), 286.

"no last word": Roland Barthes, *Barthes on Barthes*, trans. Richard Howard. University of California Press, 1994, 50.

Citations, fourteenth section
"into an imagined 'endlessness'": Robert Duncan, "Passages 33: Transmissions," *Ground Work I*, New Directions 1984, 19.

"I am not sure that is not the end." Gertrude Stein, the last line of *The Geographical History of America or the Relation of Human Nature to the Human Mind*. Johns Hopkins University Press, [1936] 1973, 235.

"So . . . " Nathaniel Mackey, *Whatsaid Serif*, City Lights Books, 1998, 14.

1. It	20. Incipit	39. Split	58. In Situ	77. Pitch Content	96. Velocity
2. She	21.Cardinals	40. One Lyric	59. Flash Back	78. Buzz Track	97. Rubrics
3. Of	22.Philadelphia Wireman	41. Of This	60. Rebus	79. Mass Observation	98. Canzone
4. In	23. Findings	42. Epistle, Studios	61. Pyx	80. Envoi	99. Intransitive
5. Gap	24.Gap	43. Gap	62. Gap	81. Gap	100. Gap
6. Midrush	25. Segno	44. Stretto	63.Dialogue of Self & Soul	82. Hinge	101. Puppet Opera
7. Me	26. M-m-ry	45. Fire	64. Forward Slash	83. Listings	102.One-on-One
8. The	27. Athwart	46. Edge	65. That	84. Juncture	103.Punctum
9. Page	28. Facing Pages	47. Printed Matter	66. Scroll	85. Hard Copy	104. The Book
X. Letters	29. Intellectual Autobiography	48. Being Astonished	67. Spirit Ditties	86. Scarpbook	105.Pilgrimage
11. Schwa	XXX. Fosse	49. Turns,& Turns, an Interpretation	68. Threshold	87. Trace Elements	106. Words
12. Diasporas	31. Serving Writ	L. Scholia & Restlessness	69. Sentences	88. X-Posting	107.Meant to say
13. Haibun	32. Renga	51. Clay Songs	LXX. Lexicon	89. Interro-gation	108. Ballad and Gloss
14. Conjunctions	33. Deixis	52. Midrash	71.Head- lines with Spoils	XC. Excess	109. Wall Newspaper
15. Little	34. Recto	53. Eclogue	72. Nanifesto	91. Proverbs	CX. Primer
16. Title	35. Verso	54. Tilde	73. Vertigo	92. Translocation	111. Arte Povera
17. Unnamed	36. Cento	55. Quiptych	74. Wanderer	93. Romantic Fragment Poem	112. Verge
18. Traduction	37. Praedelle	56. Bildungs-gedicht with Apple	75. Doggerel	94. Mail Art	113. Index
19. Working Conditions	38. Georgics & Shadow	57. Workplace, Nekuia	76. Work Table with Scale Models	95. Erg	114.Exergue and Volta

Unnumbered, Précis (after 57, before 58)